Get The Job You Love

An easy to follow guide to help students get the career they want

Marjorie Weingrow
Award-Winning UC Berkeley Career Advisor

Disclaimer
This book is designed to provide accurate and
authoritative information with regard to finding the
right career and job.

The purpose is not to cover the whole subject, but
to present a proven approach based on professional
experience and the coaching and mentoring of hundreds of university students. The author urges you
to learn as much as you can by studying, practicing,
and consulting with career counselors.

Every effort has been made to make these materials
easy to understand and follow. Use the techniques
and tools as a general guide and not as the ultimate
or exclusive source of information. The author may
not be held liable or responsible to any person or
entity with respect to loss or damage caused, or
alleged to be caused, directly or indirectly by the
information contained herein. The names and characteristics of all the people used as examples have
been altered to protect their privacy.

This book is sold with the understanding that the
author is not engaged in rendering any type of legal
or financial advice. If legal, financial and other expert
advice and assistance are required, the services of
competent professionals should be sought.

Inneract Project's mission is to introduce
underserved youth to careers in design by
providing free classes, mentorship and support
for higher education.

Learn About Us:
Visit us at inneractproject.org or "like" us at
Facebook.com/inneractproject

Acknowledgments

This book could not have been created without the help of Tresa Eyres – my mentor, friend, coach and extraordinary wordsmith, who helped me get this book from my head to paper.

Jim Horan, who put the idea in my head and gave me the boot and confidence to get going AND finish!

My son, Daniel, who always has confidence in me and inspires me every day.

I'm incredibly grateful to all the SAGE Scholars who were open and ready to go out of their comfort zones and find the jobs they love.

Illustrations by Inneract Project students, Olivia Nevins-Carbins and Taylor Leong

Please visit:
www.thejobyoulove.com

Marjorie Weingrow is the Executive Director of the University of California at Berkeley SAGE Scholars Program, an experiential leadership development program she initiated in 1999 to assist low-income undergraduates learn and practice the professional skills they need to get the jobs they love. Marjorie also has over 20 years of experience in business. In the private and nonprofit business sectors, she implemented many successful internship programs, focusing on helping students in low-income, underserved communities.

Marjorie is the recipient of the UC Berkeley Chancellor's Outstanding Staff Award, as well as a recipient of the Jefferson Award for excellence in community service.

She was Chair of the Business and Leadership Forum of the San Francisco Commonwealth Club and received certification from the Leadership Training division of the Coaches Training Institute. Marjorie also has extensive experience working with leaders in the area of human potential using experiential, rather than theoretical practices. She has worked with many businesses helping them train their workforce.

Marjorie is a sought after presenter and workshop leader focusing on inspirational leadership development. She has been a keynote speaker at the San Francisco Commonwealth Club and the Craigslist Foundation Annual Conference. She has been featured on the ABC News, television's Beyond the Headlines, and has also been featured in the *San Francisco Chronicle* and the *East Bay Business Times.*

Her passion is working with people to help them excel in their careers in doing the work they love.

Contents

Introduction

Employers are hiring! There's a job out there that you'll love. Even in the worst job market, companies and organizations have to continue to find good candidates in order to stay competitive. Of course when the economic situation is bad, employers expect employees to work more and be able to prove their worth; however, no organization can continue to be effective if it doesn't hire the right people. According to the National Association of Colleges and Employers' 2011 Student Survey, the median time that seniors from the class of 2011 took to get a job was 7.74 months, so start cracking now!!! You need to be prepared.

This book is about how you as a student can effectively compete for a job you'll love in the career of your choice. As an undergraduate or graduate student with little or no professional career experience, you may wonder what you have to offer and how to find the right job at a good salary.

Although this book is specifically intended for you as a college or university student seeking internships or your first professional position after graduation, the same principles – and many of the proven practices and success tips – apply to the career and job changes you'll make throughout your working life.

Many people will tell you how challenging the job situation is and that you won't find a good, well-paying job. The reality is that many people are being hired. You need to have the attitude that you can do it and you will get the job that you love. This book is designed to help you and encourage you, but the positive attitude has to be yours!

What You'll Learn

This book leads you through the process needed. For best results, study the book and complete the activities in chapter order. As needed, return to the chapters that are most relevant for you.

Chapter 1 covers how to identify a satisfying career. If you've already chosen one, it will help you confirm your decision or understand the need to change direction.

Chapters 2 through 5 cover how to prepare for your role in professional employment, how to develop a marketing portfolio, and how to identify the right job opportunities to pursue.

Chapters 6 and 7 cover "the how" of getting and acing the interview and finalizing your salary and benefits with negotiation skills.

Throughout the book, common and helpful components are:

- Proven, measurable actions you can take

- Questions to guide you

- What you can ask for

- How to follow up

The first thing you need to know ...

What every employer is looking for in every new hire and every employee.

The Successful E³ Professional

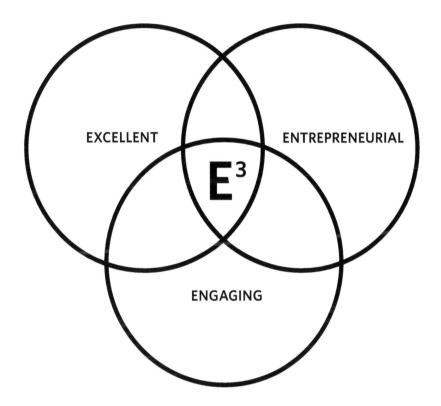

Regardless of the career field, the specific organization, or the job title, employers are seeking three key attributes in employees they hire and retain. As a job candidate, and later as an employee, you must demonstrate that you are Entrepreneurial, Excellent and Engaging, or "E" to the third power – "E³."

It is these same three attributes that work for savvy job seekers who find and get the right job in the career they want.

1. Used by permission from Donald Hanratty, Ron Biagi, Tresa Eyres, authors of "Manage Your Own Career: Make it a SNAPP" ©2002, It's The How Publications. Permission to use E³ concept must be requested from the authors.

MEANINGS OF THE ATTRIBUTES

Excellent

Your professional and technical skills must be current and of the highest quality, and you must be able to demonstrate the results you have achieved. To be truly excellent, you must not only be constantly learning more and gaining new skills, but also making your knowledge useful and sharing it effectively with others. You must be 100% responsible and dependable in meeting assigned goals – and frequently "going the extra mile."

Your resume and bio must clearly showcase your academic record, abilities with new technology, your work experience, and leadership abilities.

Entrepreneurial

You must demonstrate your ability to manage your job in the way an entrepreneur builds a business. It means keeping an eye on global events, industry trends, and what's going on with the competition. It requires being strategic, credible, and doing everything necessary and appropriate to get results. You must be able to inspire others with your vision and execution.

The number one way to find and get the job you'll love is to develop and nurture a strong network of professionals who are willing to assist you. Doing that requires you to be strategic, credible, persistent, and to give back as much as you may ask.

You will demonstrate your entrepreneurial skills to prospective employers as you interview and negotiate the job agreement.

Engaging

You must know how to work with others, leading by example regardless of your position on the team. You must be respectful, courteous, and dependable. You need to be approachable, diplomatic and communicative. In other words, you must get along well with others so they'll like you, want to work with you, and follow your lead when it's appropriate.

Attracting others to your team requires you to be respectful, courteous, dependable, approachable, diplomatic, and communicative. You must show your professionalism in every communication with prospective employers and interview flawlessly, including your ability to get along with a wide range of co-workers.

How can you tell if you're "E³"?

Following are the key attributes every successful employee needs to develop and what you'll need to show as you search for the right career and job for you.

You will know you're Excellent when ...

- You stay informed about trends and developments in your field.

- You often serve as the go-to person for answers.

- You're up to date on the latest technology.

- You serve as leader or key member on teams.

- You consistently do exceptional work completing projects on time, within budget.

- You initiate and implement ways to make money, save money, save time, reduce risk, etc.

You will know you're Entrepreneurial when ...

- People describe you as an out-of-the-box thinker.

- You contribute valuable and innovative ideas.

- You take initiative to solve problems resulting in measurable, value-added change.

- You get involved with professional associations.

- Coworkers seek out and act on your suggestions.

- People come to you for advice and direction.

You will know you're Engaging when...

- You take time to explain things to others.

- You return phone messages and e-mails within 24 hours.

- You deliver on your promises, even when it's inconvenient.

- You regularly provide helpful feedback that is genuinely appreciated.

- You listen and learn from feedback others give to you.

- You are often among the first few chosen to join a team.

- You keep in touch with a large group of colleagues.

- You can negotiate and mediate problems amicably.

- You provide frequent praise and support.

- You collaborate with people of different nationalities, races, beliefs, cultures, organizations etc. to identify similarities and appreciate differences.

Get started today!

"A goal is a dream with a deadline!"

If you've been working at the same time you are a student, performing volunteer work while maintaining a solid grade point average in school and developing strong relationships throughout your lifetime, you have a head start at finding the professional job you want after graduation. If you are missing any of those steps, it's not too late to begin.

Regardless of where you are now, this book will help you with techniques and success tips at every step of your career and job search process. You can find the career of your dreams with the salary you deserve!

Finding a job is like finding a parking space; all you need is one good one.

CHAPTER 1

Finding the Right Career for YOU!

You'll know you've found it when ...

you are excited about the contribution you make to the organization and/or society, you're willing to persevere through significant challenges to reach your career goal, and time doesn't seem to exist when you are working. It's important to remember what is important to YOU.

Figure out what's important to you by answering the following questions. Record your answers and refer to them periodically. Your answers will probably change over time.

Career-wise, what are my non-negotiables (what I must have or do and what I won't do)?

1. **What must I do? What I LOVE!**

_____

_____

_____

_____

2. **What I won't do or makes me crazy doing?**

_____

_____

_____

_____

3. **What is most important to me ... being useful, creative or productive?**

_____

_____

_____

_____

4. **What am I good at or love to do that I want to do more?**

_____

_____

_____

5. **Where will I be working? (location, size of organization, physical attributes, in/outdoors, dress criteria, mission, values).**

_____

_____

_____

_____

6. **Who will I be working with? Working alone or with limited numbers of co-workers? Managing people?**

_____

_____

_____

_____

7. **Write your career vision statement. (Writing it is essential.)**

    Example: When I'm _____ (what) in _____ (what kind of organization) working with_____ (people, information, ideas, tools, etc.) time doesn't exist.

_____

_____

_____

_____

_____

_____

_____

_____

Find people in the profession or career area that you want to explore.

Ask people in the field open-ended questions about their work. Typical questions can be:

- What were the important steps in reaching this point in your career?

- What do you like and dislike about your career?

- On a daily or weekly basis, how do you spend most of your time?

Following your informational interviews, review your notes and, if needed, revise your vision statement.

Ask yourself if this is still the career you want. If yes, share your vision only with people you're sure will support you. (Do not share this vision yet with people who may not encourage your ideas.) If it isn't the career you still want, go back and repeat actions 1 through 7 at any time.

Follow up: As you gather more information and begin your job search, revisit your vision. Continue to ask yourself if this career is still what you want and why you may or may not want to pursue it. Don't let job availability or the economy deter you right away. Companies and organizations are hiring people every day, especially those who are passionate about what they do.

Passions and Gifts Activity

The purpose of this activity is to help you identify what drives you to take actions and what contributions you have to offer.

Read the sentences below. Check all that you believe strongly apply to you. One blank space in each list has been added, but feel free to add or change things as they apply to you.

I LOVE TO...

- ❏ Lead and create teams
- ❏ Solve problems
- ❏ Create opportunities from challenges (produce, achieve, create)
- ❏ _____

I AM PASSIONATE ABOUT...

- ❏ Taking on big challenges
- ❏ Achieving results
- ❏ Working with people rather than on my own
- ❏ _____

I AM EXCITED ABOUT...

- ❏ Completing a challenging situation
- ❏ Being able to do what no one else seems to be able to do
- ❏ Seeing people grow, do more than was ever expected
- ❏ Being the best—person, team, organization
- ❏ _____

WHAT I REALLY LIKE IS...

- ❏ Working with very bright people who have good values
- ❏ Working with organizations that are respected or where respect can be created
- ❏ Building a culture that will succeed and be a place where people can grow and enjoy work
- ❏ _____

MY GREATEST CONTRIBUTION IS ...

- ☐ Being able to do many different things well
- ☐ Exceeding expectations
- ☐ Saving the day – taking on bad situations, fixing them, and turning them into winners
- ☐ _____

I AM GOOD AT ...

- ☐ Communication – and can express myself very well
- ☐ Motivating others
- ☐ Getting the job done quickly with practical, interesting solutions
- ☐ _____

I AM KNOWN FOR ...

- ☐ My leadership abilities
- ☐ Overcoming challenging obstacles
- ☐ My good humor and personality
- ☐ Seeing the "big picture" – issues, problems, solutions, outcomes
- ☐ Getting to the heart of the matter quickly and intuitively analyzing the situation
- ☐ _____

I HAVE AN EXCEPTIONAL ABILITY TO ...

- ☐ Be creative
- ☐ Take complex problems and quickly develop solutions
- ☐ Motivate others
- ☐ _____

Directions for this segment:

Complete the following sentences as candidly as you can. Feel free to provide multiple answers to each question or skip ones that you feel you can't answer yet. Keep your responses focused on career aspects of your life (as opposed to your personal or social life, etc.). Review your answers after a day or so to refine or expand them.

What's important to you about a career? _____

_____

_____

I feel passionate about ... _____

_____

_____

I am excited about ... _____

_____

_____

What I really like is ... _____

_____

_____

My greatest contribution is ... _____

_____

_____

I am particularly good at ... _____

_____

_____

I am known for ... _____

_____

_____

I have an exceptional ability to ... _____

_____

_____

People often ask for my help with ... _____

_____

_____

What motivates me most is ... _____

_____

_____

I would feel disappointed, frustrated or sad if I couldn't ... _____

_____

_____

Directions for this segment:

After you've reviewed and refined your answers (previous page), ask these important questions and write down your answers in detail.

How do your personal gifts, goals and passions correspond/align with your career focus?_____

_____

_____

_____

_____

_____

What implications do these answers have for your career choices?_____

_____

_____

_____

_____

_____

What is one thing you can do starting today to enhance or change your career focus so it will be more in tune with your true passions and gifts?

_____

_____

_____

_____

CHAPTER 2
Making the Right Impression

Appearing "professional" is essential before you can make a great impression with people who can help you. What does it mean to be "professional?" Some words to think about are skilled, trained, and confident. It's someone who always does what he/she promises. A true professional is "E³": excellent, entrepreneurial, and engaging.

You'll know you've made a great impression when ... people you're talking with are asking you questions, when they are offering suggestions and resources, and offering you their business cards. There's an excitement in the mutual sharing of ideas and interests.

Sometimes making the right impression with the right person is a coincidence – a chance encounter that leads you to a promising job opportunity. More often, you must plan ahead.

1. Prepare a captivating sound bite or "pitch"

This is two or three sentences that create enthusiasm from the person you're meeting to want to know more. It's important that you show enthusiasm when you deliver your pitch. Your pitch can have three parts:

- Your name – first and last, said clearly and slowly, especially if you have an unusual name

- A fact about your work or your course of study

- Something insightful or interesting about your work or study that will lead the other person to ask a question

Examples that should lead to the other person asking questions:

I'm Joe Smith. My major at Boston University is Business. I'm really excited about working with people in the financial industry to help people understand complex financial risks.

- OR -

I'm Robin Brown. My field is engineering. I'm really interested in meeting people in the engineering profession to see what kind of jobs are available in this field.

- OR -

Someone interested in changing a career focus

I'm Leticia Lee. Currently I'm an accountant at a big law firm, but I'm interested in exploring opportunities for a small non-profit.

Activity 2-1: Create your pitch

Hello, I'm _____

Something about your work or your course of study:

_____

What's going to spark interest that will lead the other person to ask a question? (Examples could be how many students are in your major, what you just found out about the major or careers in the major, etc. why you're interested in this course of study now.)

_____

_____

_____

2. Practice your enthusiastic pitch

Say your pitch out loud to yourself with enthusiasm until you can say it clearly and naturally. Concentrate on saying your pitch as confident and compelling statements. Remember to smile – it will also help you relax.

Avoid using an upward inflection in your voice when you are not asking a question. Upward inflections at the end of a statement will make you sound less confident and is common among students. You probably won't hear it yourself if you do it, but always be ready and thankful for feedback.

Consider asking a friend to watch and point it out to you.

Activity 2-2: Practice delivering your pitch with confidence

Mindful practice will help you deliver your pitch in confidence when it counts the most.

- Say your pitch to a mirror.

    ▲ Are you looking yourself in the eye and smiling? (See Activity 2-3)

    ▲ Do you sound confident?

- Say your pitch to a trusted family member or friend who will give honest feedback.

    ▲ Smile.

    ▲ Shake hands with a firm but not bone-crushing grip.

    ▲ Speak with confidence.

    ▲ Maintain eye contact.

    ▲ Pause and wait for reaction.

    ▲ Ask for feedback about your smile, handshake, pitch, and eye contact. Ask for clarification and suggestions. Listen to the response, take note, and

    ▲ Practice, Practice, Practice!

Repeat until your sound bite feels natural, engaging, and enthusiastic.

3. Dress and act as professionals do

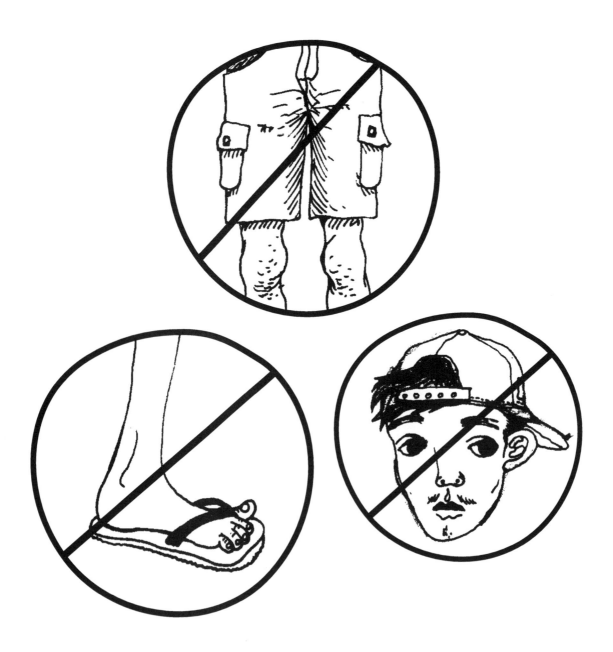

First impressions are lasting, so you want to project "professional" within the first five seconds. That's how little time first impressions take. You want the focus on who you are, what you're saying, and what you can do so there are no distractions due to inappropriate dress.

Prepare your clothes to dress for success

Making the right impression is not about the latest fashion. It's about dressing in a way that's consistent with you looking like a professional:

Men and Women:

- Well-fitting dark pants

- Long-sleeve, buttoned shirt

- Dark, closed-toed shoes

- Jacket or sweater

- Minimal jewelry

- Minimal or no fragrance

Men:

- Clean-shaven

Women:

- No cleavage

- No tight-fitting slacks or shirt

- No skirts above the knee

Make and maintain eye contact, *and smile*

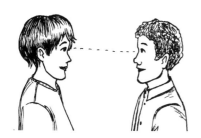

In U.S. culture, eye contact is a sign of confidence and trustworthiness. It's absolutely essential for making the right impression.

If making and keeping eye contact doesn't come easily, practice can change that.

Activity 2-3: Practice making eye contact with:

- Babies. They generally aren't shy about eye contact or staring. See how long you can keep a baby's full attention.

- Service providers such as waiters, bank tellers, retail salespeople, and medical personnel.

- Family and friends. If you feel safe doing so, tell them what you're practicing and ask them to remind you when you forget and look away.

Smile

Also in U.S. culture, smiling is a sign of confidence and friendliness. It's absolutely essential for making the right impression.

Do you have trouble smiling when meeting someone new? Practice with Activity 2-3, making sure to smile with every encounter. Even if you're nervous, remember to breathe and smile and "fake it till you make it."

Practice positive body language

Before you have a chance to tell your story, your body language tells a story about you. It says you're "open" or "closed," confident or shy, friendly or unfriendly – and people will respond accordingly.

Posture, handshakes, and mannerisms are visual clues about whether you're confident, embarrassed, shy, etc. Arms folded across your chest shows that you are guarded. Standing straight immediately shows confidence. Sitting straight at the edge of your chair while leaning in slightly, shows that you are engaged and actively listening.

Activity 2-4: Practice positive body language

- Confident posture

    ▲ Look in the mirror while standing straight, head in line with your hips, and shoulders back so your hands fall by your side.

    ▲ Close your eyes while you're in this "confident" posture so you feel it. Practice often so this will become your normal posture.

- Confident handshake

    ▲ The curve next to your thumb should hook in with the other person's to form a good secure grip. Make your grip firm, but not a cruncher. A good, firm, handshake is extremely important. It helps show your professionalism and confidence. Practice this a lot.

    ▲ If you tend to have sweaty palms, casually wipe them on your pants before shaking hands.

- Mannerisms

    ▲ Use your hands as well as facial expressions when talking.

    ▲ Be sure to maintain eye contact, and smile at appropriate times.

    ▲ Avoid fiddling with jewelry, hair, pens, pocket change or keys.

4. Perfect the art of great conversation

What is great conversation? It's the use of active listening and responding and talking – in that order. Great conversations are beautiful "works of heart," with all parties equally hearing and being heard.

Great conversationalists know that others like to be heard and understood, so they actively listen and respond when others are doing the talking. They are genuinely interested in other people. They ask more than tell, and listen to learn.

And great conversationalists do more than listen; they have knowledge and interests that others want to hear about.

Demonstrating that you are a great conversationalist will go far in making a great impression. The following are some tips and activities to help you gain skill in participating in a great conversation.

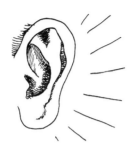

Active listening

Great conversations are cooperative, not competitive; they are characterized by attention-giving as well as attention-getting. Active listening is a gift you give to others.

Activity 2-5: Proactive listening

Practice listening to someone in person without asking questions. Maintain eye contact, nod your head appropriately, and when finished, ask an appropriate question about what was said that requires an answer that will be more than yes or no. Be careful not to make it about you and referring to your own experience.

Stay totally engaged with the person the entire time whether you are listening or talking.

Verbal response

The response you give to another's talk can take two forms: the "shift-response" and the "support-response." The support-response keeps attention on the speaker's topic. The shift-response moves attention away from the speaker and draws attention to the listener.

Example of shift response

Person 1: I'm thinking of changing majors.

Person 2: I did that last year. I was tired of finance, so I started taking social science courses. I think I want to be a research psychologist.

In this case, Person 2 used the topic Person 1 initiated to shift the topic to himself.

How is that disrespectful?

How could you keep this conversation going and keep it about Person 1?

Example of support response

Person 1: I'm thinking of changing majors.

Person 2: That's interesting. What are you thinking of instead?

Person 1: I'm thinking of changing from accounting to biotech.

Person 2: That's a great field. My brother is a scientist at Merck – he loves it. Would you be interested in talking to him about opportunities in the field?

In this case, Person 2 used the topic to support Person 1's idea.

How is this keeping Person 1 involved and engaged?

How could you continue moving this conversation forward?

Activity 2-6: Enquire and expand on others' information and ideas

As the other person shares a story or explains an idea, enquire to show interest

- What
- Why
- Who
- When
- Where
- How

You don't need to ask them all of these every time. Listen for some point that calls for more explanation, and ask a question.

To show you've been actively listening, attempt to rephrase and integrate what you've learned into a new situation. *Examples:* "So what I think you're suggesting is ..." or "I believe you're referring to the application process on line being done this way ..."

Talking

Great conversation occurs when all parties are respectfully sharing information and ideas more or less equally. When people talk too much or talk too little, conversations are less satisfying.

TRY TO AVOID THESE TWO COMMON MISTAKES:

Talking too much

We've all been in uncomfortable conversations with people who talk too much. People who talk too much give the impression that they don't care about the other person.

Two common reasons for talking too much:

1. The need to "think out loud."

2. Lack of ease (nervousness) in a particular social or business setting.

Here's how to tell if you talk too much and if so, some ideas about how to change.

Activity 2-7: Test to see if you talk too much and what to do about it

Answer these questions with "yes" or "no:"

- I've been told by family, friends, teachers, or employers that I talk too much.

- When I'm talking, people say "uh huh," but don't appear to be listening or engaged in what I'm saying.

- It feels like I'm talking to myself because people stop asking questions or adding information to what I'm saying.

- People interrupt me when I'm in the middle of sentences.

- People stop making eye contact and begin looking around for a way to escape.

If you answered "yes," try:

- Being mindful that you may be talking too much in social and professional situations.

- Remembering elementary school playground rules and taking turns with others. Toss the ball to another player; soon enough it will come back to you.

- Practicing active listening and asking good questions. (See Activities 2-5 and 2-6.)

Note: There are incurable "talkers" who will talk on and on despite the best attempts of others. When you come across someone who does this, politely end the conversation by saying you need to talk to someone before he leaves or you need to meet someone.

Talking too little

We've all been in uncomfortable conversations with people who talk too little. We often make false assumptions about such people, assuming they are boring, lack intelligence, or have no interest in us or are extremely shy.

Two common reasons why people talk too little:

1. Lack of knowledge about the subject under discussion.

2. Lack of self-confidence, assuming that others will not be interested in them or their ideas and views.

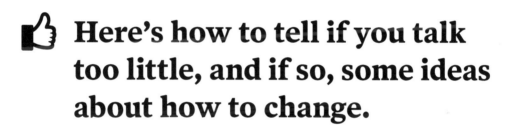

Here's how to tell if you talk too little, and if so, some ideas about how to change.

Activity 2-8: Test to see if you talk too little

Answer these questions with "yes" or "no:"

- People tell me I'm very quiet.

- I'm shy.

- After a few minutes of talking with me, people begin looking around for a way to end the conversation.

- When in a group of 3 or more, I feel almost invisible as others take over the conversation.

- I'd rather stay home than talk to strangers in a social or business situation.

If you answered "yes:"

- Start becoming an industry expert by reading newsletters, blogs and relevant association information.

- Be informed by keeping up on current events – news of your community and the world, trends in your career field, sports, music, and entertainment. Read or listen to books. Attend lectures where you can learn something and meet people.

- Practice talking to strangers in a safe environment such as stores, restaurants, and offices where service providers are likely to respond in friendly ways. Smile, make eye contact, and ask for recommendations about what to eat, drink, wear, or what to do. Respond with a thank you and how you intend to use the recommendation. Volunteer some relevant information of your own.

- Compliments are great conversation starters. Be specific with your compliment (it will make someone's day). Be sure to make eye contact and smile. Give a specific thank-you rather than just "thanks." (See Activity 2-9.)

- Practice active listening and asking good questions that require more than a yes or no answer. (See Activities 2-5 and 2-6.)

- Ask strategic questions that can allow you to interject ideas and experiences of your own. *Example:* What was your major? (The answer to the question may allow you to interject something interesting that you've learned.)

If shyness is your issue, start a conversation with a specific question. Then follow up with your thoughts and ideas.

Activity 2-9: Say a specific "thank you"

Sincere compliments or thank yous are great conversation starters – if you make them specific.

EXAMPLE AT A COFFEE SHOP:

You: It's so hot outside today ... I think I'll have the iced coffee. Are you selling more of that today than usual?

Barrista: We can hardly keep up with the demand!

You: Thank you for the great service and the great coffee! I always know I'll have good customer experience here.

The beauty of a thank you is in the specifics. Try this:

Write the name of one person to give a specific "thank you" today:

_____

Write the specific thing that deserves a thank you (doing something for me, giving something to someone else or me, being kind, forgiving, helping, etc.):_____

_____

_____

Write how that specific thing makes you feel: _____

_____

_____

Say all three parts to the other person in a natural, conversational style.

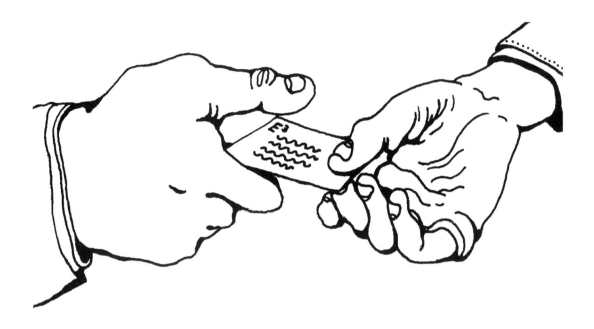

5. Close the conversation and follow up

Be respectful. Rather than take up too much of a person's time, you'll make a better impression by closing the conversation and following up by email, letter, or phone call. Busy people get lots of emails, so don't forget about using the phone!

Close the conversation

Closing a conversation can feel awkward. Here are two ways to end the exchange gracefully once you feel you've made a meaningful connection.

"I know there are other people here waiting to talk with you. I don't want to take up all your time now, but I'd love to discuss this further. I have your card now, and you have mine. What is the best way to follow up with you – by phone or email?"

or ...

"This has been so helpful. I'd love to talk with you more about this. May I have your card? What is the best way to follow up – by phone or email?"

Business card etiquette

Always carry business cards. Free business cards are available on the internet and can also be easily made on your printer with business cardstock from any office supply store. You don't need to have a title or work for an organization to use a business card. Include all of your pertinent contact information, and also include your website if you have one.

Offer cards only to people you've spoken to and have made a connection.

Follow up

Let the other person know when and how you will follow up, and always be timely. Follow-up should be within 24 hours after the meeting.

About your voice mail message:

Now is the time to re-evaluate your voice mail message. Let go of any music, rap, slang or any kind of unprofessional message. Your message should be concise and clearly spoken.

Example:

> *Hello – this is Susan Robertson. Please leave me a message and I'll call you back as soon as possible. Thank you.*

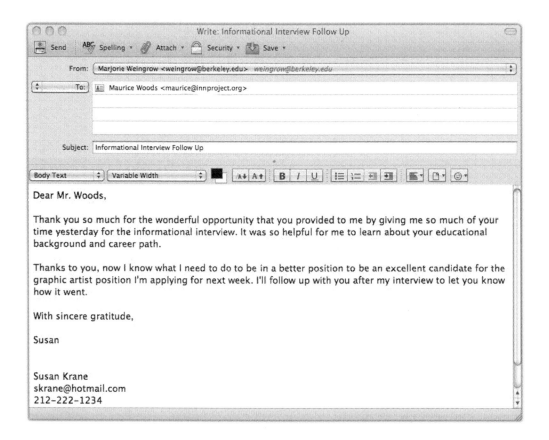

About your email message:

This is also the time to create a new email address if yours isn't easy or is inappropriate for professional purposes. Simple is always best for an email address. Don't use a long address like John.W.Simonson.Jr.45789@hotmail.com, and never use anything like slickguy@berkeley.edu.

Include a signature template in your email which appears after you write your name at the end. Email programs allow you to create one that will automatically appear at the bottom of all of the messages you create.

Here's an example of a signature template:

———————

John Johnson
(212)427-5438
jjohnson@nyu.edu
Biology Major, Class of 2014

Always create a subject line that's helpful such as Alumni Meeting Follow Up or Internship Application Attached. When people get too many emails they scan their subject lines. Emails without subject content often go to trash.

Never use acronoyms in your email or letters unless you're positive your reader knows what the acronym means.

Calling or writing your first email follow up should always be professional. Never start with "Hey John" and if you don't know the person, don't write "How're you doing?" Remember to be concise, simple and professional. When sending an email ALWAYS use good grammar and punctuation, and reread your email message before you click "send." When leaving a phone message speak clearly, especially if you have an unusual name. Say your phone number slowly and then repeat it.

Example of a first follow-up (email or phone call)

Dear or Hello _____: (Use either the first name if you are on first name basis, or Mr./Ms. Don't make the mistake of writing Dear John Smith. This is unprofessional and sounds like a form letter).

We spoke at the _____ event. I enjoyed hearing about _____.

I would love to be part of/hear more about/discuss further _____. I wonder if you have time within the next few days/weeks. My schedule is open on

_____.

Thank you again for your time and willingness to _____

_____

Best regards,

If you receive no response to the first message, follow up at least two more times. Also, don't forget about using the phone! So many people are overburdened with emails.

Example of a second follow-up contact

Dear _____:

We spoke at the _____ event. I want you to know I've been following your helpful suggestion to _____ and as a result _____ (indicate some progress).

If you have any additional information or advice, I will appreciate the opportunity to _____, and I look forward to meeting you/hearing from you whenever it's convenient.

After two weeks, if you have received no response, make one last try.

Example of a third follow-up contact

Dear _____:

I'm sorry to bother you again. I don't want to be a pest, so let me know if you would prefer that I not email you. I was thinking that you might be busy or out of town, so if we could follow up, I'd really appreciate it.

Chapter 2 Reminders

To build skill, you will need to do more than read this chapter. Experts say it takes regular practice at least three weeks before changes become habits.

Some of the skill practice activities in this chapter are habits you may already use. Others involve change in behaviors that are based on old beliefs and will take effort to change.

Review the reminders below. Check the ones you need to practice. Then practice over the next weeks and months. Do not try to change everything at once, but work on a few at a time.

Sections 1 and 2:

- ❏ Create a compelling pitch or sound bite.
- ❏ Practice delivering it.

Section 3: Dress and act like a professional

- ❏ Prepare an outfit to dress for success.
- ❏ Practice smiling and maintaining eye contact.
- ❏ Practice confident body language.

Section 4: Perfect the art of great conversation

- ❏ Practice active listening by enquiring and enlarging on others' information and ideas.
- ❏ Check whether you talk too much or too little.

Section 5: Close the conversation and follow up

- ❏ Practice gracefully closing conversations.
- ❏ Ask for business cards, and follow up within 24 hours.
- ❏ Prepare and always carry your own business cards.
- ❏ Follow up meaningful connections by phone or email.
- ❏ Follow up two more times if there's no response.

CHAPTER 3

Building the Right Relationships

Approximately

75%

of jobs are found through networking.

Networking to build relationships is the best way to develop leads to the jobs you are most likely to want. Approximately 75% of jobs are found through networking.

We've all heard the expression, "It's not what you know, it's who you know." Your "know how" is important – it is part of being Excellent. "Who knows you" is equally important – that's the result of being Entrepreneurial and Engaging.

You'll know you're successful when ... people you meet are willing and able to help guide you toward your career goals.

1. Build your professional network

Your personal networks probably include family, friends, your religious organization, your neighborhood, sports team, and other university contacts or organizations. Most important is your school's alumni association. You can usually join the alumni association before you graduate.

As you start finding the career and the job you want, you'll need to develop your professional network. While some people in your existing personal network may also become part of your growing professional network, you need to recruit a lot more new contacts.

What does "professional networking" mean?
It's relationship building!

Successful professional networking is the ongoing development of mutually satisfying and beneficial relationships that can last for only a short time or as long as many years. Members of networks come and go, depending on mutual needs and changing priorities. Often, members of personal and professional networks cross lines.

What is the best way to network?

Spend as much time as possible networking both on and off campus. Use the internet and network in person too.

On-line networking

There are a number of internet sites that promote networking. One of the best-known and accepted professional networking sites is LinkedIn. LinkedIn and Facebook are covered in Chapter 4. You should also use Google+ and Twitter.

In-person networking

In addition to on-line networking, it's very important to start and continue face-to-face networking. Chances are you'll get a greater return on your time investment when you're making in-person connections.

Who should your professional network include?

Your professional network ideally will include people who:

- Have expertise and contacts in the professional world and/or your chosen career

- Are acknowledged leaders in their fields

- Have the capacity to guide and mentor others

- Are generous with their time and talents, candid and gracious in their feedback

Note: Professional networking is meant to be reciprocal. People you enlist should be those people you will be happy to return the favor. You're probably thinking that you don't have much to offer at this stage in your life; however, always ask if there's something you can do to help them. It can be something easy for you like explaining Facebook features.

2. Give in return for what you get through networking

The best long-standing, solid networking relationships are built on a foundation of mutual give and take.

As a young person who is beginning to develop a professional network, you are looking for professionals who can support you with information, introductions, referrals, leads, and possibly even work.

What benefits, you may be wondering, can you offer in return to these helpful people so that a solid relationship can be built and maintained? There are things you can do both in the short and long term.

What you can offer in the short term

Professionals who are willing to give you the gift of their knowledge, connections, and support are people who enjoy helping others. With the exception of expressed appreciation, they probably are not thinking about what they will get in return.

The very minimum should be a thank-you within 24 hours.

Here are some ways to express your gratitude that go beyond the minimum and that will help ensure that the relationship will be positive:

- Send a hand-written note that is specific about how you used their gift of knowledge, experience or connection and what it means to you.

- As appropriate, publicly acknowledge your appreciation when introducing the person to another colleague.

- Send an email or card with a personal message reiterating your gratitude – even months later.

- Keep the giver apprised of your progress toward your goal. After the initial thank-you, send periodic short email updates that also reiterate your appreciation. Too often, givers are thanked immediately and then they never again hear back.

What you can offer in the long term

The long term applies to some future date when you are well-established in your job and career. Here are some things you can provide in the long-term to valued professionals in your network:

- Stay in touch by email, phone, and/or in-person (and not just when you need a favor). These are personal "touches," not mass emails or updates on social media.

- When opportunities arise, send topical industry news, employment opportunities and/or business leads you know the person will appreciate.

- When your services are required, offer them at reduced or no charge as appropriate.

- Introduce the person to others in your professional network.

- Let the person know that, thanks to his/her example, you are sharing your expertise and contacts with others.

Almost everyone feels awkward or uneasy at first, but networking is the most important skill you can develop when starting your career AND furthering your career.

Activity 3-1 leads you through the process of identifying people you already know who are members of your professional network.

Activity 3-1: Inventory your existing networks

- Create a table or spreadsheet like the one on the next page. Change the categories (School, Community, etc.) depending on your network.

- Be sure to add a category for professional contacts, even if you can't think of anyone to list now.

- Next to each name, record contact information, the date you have contacted or will make a contact. Include a column for comments to remind you of the status of your contact.

Table 3-1: Professional Network Contact List

	Relationship	Contact info	Contact Date	Comments
School				
A.B. Smith	HS Chem teacher	smith@columbus.edu	05/10/14	Retired – email returned
VJ Stein	HS guidance counselor	stein@king.edu	06/24/14	Sent friendly email
Dr. C.T. Close	Psych Prof	carclose@nyu.edu	01/24/15	On vacation – follow up
Community				
GW Bowen	Church pastor	gwb@church.net	07/14/15	Friendly email – promises to put the word out
EM Schiller	Rotary	ems@clorox.com	10/2/15	Agreed to be a reference
Career Professionals				
R.R Lopez	Campus career office	rrlopez@sfstate.edu	11/11/16	Info about job fairs
Professionals				
KL Chang	Toastmasters 03/24/12	klchang@macys.com	03/26/12	Seemed interested in my ambitions -- get in touch after graduation
J Samos	Toastmasters 07/14/15	joansamos@corp.com	07/19/15	Has contact at Science Labs
Chris Cross	Technology Meetup 12/11/15	ccross@abc.com	12/15/15	Asked for referral for informational interview. Waiting reply. F/U 1/3/16

Where do you find more people?

Since personal connections are
the most effective way to build a
professional network, you must
go out and make face-to-face
connections where you can meet
as many professionals as possible.
Through alumni resources, colleges
and universities offer opportunities.
Student-run professional organizations
are another way to recruit and meet
professionals. Table 3-2 will start
you thinking about places you can
go to begin developing beneficial
contacts, but do not be limited by these
suggestions.

Table 3-2 Networking locations

Organization or Opportunity	Notes	What Can I Do
Professional associations such as communications, law, technology, medicine, etc.	Associations often offer student rates for members.	Go to career center
Conventions for professionals	Fees can be high. Sometimes students can volunteer in lieu of entrance fees.	Ask professors or teachers about professional organizations in your area
Community centers and other non-profit organizations	Most metropolitan areas have volunteer bureaus or centers. Identify one or two – political, social, educational, etc. You will meet volunteers and business professionals. You can often gain experience and contacts in your chosen field.	Go on line to see the community calendar or check the local newspapers
Public library	Find free lectures in topics of interest. Network with the other participants and use your captivating sound bite to introduce yourself to the speaker and other guests.	Check their website
Book stores	Find free lectures by authors of books about your field of interest. Network with the other participants and use your compelling pitch to introduce yourself to the author.	Events often are posted on-line and in newspapers
Toastmasters International	A great and inexpensive resource throughout the country, use it to build skills with public speaking while adding contacts to your professional network.	Find out where they meet in your area at toastmasters.org
Religious and political organizations	Typically, many members are professional people.	
Events open to the public	Art shows, auto shows, public lectures are often free. Network.	Internet, community and city websites
Meetups	Meetups are face-to-face interest groups on topics ranging from candle-making to high-tech marketing.	Go to www.meetup.com, enter a topic and your zip code
Service organizations	Rotary International, for example, sponsors clubs called Rotaract for people aged 18 – 30. Many Rotaract clubs meet on college campuses.	

3. Go out to meet people

Once you identify where to meet potential members of your professional network, you must get out and build relationships. Events planned specifically for networking are one example, but any gathering can provide opportunities. Locate opportunities in or near the place you live or go to school.

Gatherings let you practice your networking skills multiple times in a single day or evening. You'll know you've been successful when you leave with at least one strong connection to follow up. Once you've found one good connection, you may be tempted to stop. Don't! What feels like a good connection may not carry through afterward, so keep going. It's also great to have choices rather than just one prospect. Keep "working the room." As you practice, you'll gain confidence.

The more contacts you acquire and follow up, the better your odds of making a great connection. Sometimes you may even end up with a great friend.

Activity 3-2: Prepare for the networking opportunity or event

Try never to just "show up." Prepare with these essential to-dos:

- ❏ Use Table 3-2 to identify events and add events or groups to join.
- ❏ Research the event, organization, and/or likely attendees. View the website, review brochures, reports, bios, newsletters, etc.
- ❏ Identify a goal for the outcome you want (i.e., minimum 2 opportunities for informational interviews with professionals in your field).
- ❏ Dress for success (see Chapter 2).
- ❏ Practice your compelling pitch (see Chapter 2).
- ❏ Carry plenty of business cards in a pocket, or anywhere that's easy to access (so you don't have to dig for a card when asked).
- ❏ If you're nervous about attending, ask a friend to accompany you – but agree not to stick together through the entire event. Tell your goal to your friend (so you'll be more likely to achieve it).
- ❏ Plan transportation so you arrive on time.
- ❏ Be well-fed before you go, even when food will be served. It's difficult to shake hands and talk when trying to juggle plates and glassware, chew and swallow.
- ❏ Don't drink alcohol; you may say and do things that won't make the right impression, and people will remember.
- ❏ Follow the tips for working a room.

Tips for working a room

- Be engaging and use your conversational skills (review Chapter 2).

- A good way to start a conversation is by asking people what brings them to the event. Is this their first time? What do you like about this group, or the meeting, or the location?

- Gracefully close conversations when it's time to move on. This happens when either you or the other person disengages. Stay tuned to the other person's body language. See if they start looking around or stop being enthusiastic. Recognize that not everyone will be a good fit for your professional network. See Chapter 2 for suggestions.

- Try not to judge and discard people too quickly – especially based on appearance or when someone is standing alone. When you engage, you may be pleasantly surprised.

- To join a small group already in conversation, stand nearby and listen for a time. When there's a break, say something like, "I hope it's alright that I've been listening in. May I add something?"

- Play the role of gracious host or hostess, even when you're not the organizer. You can build confidence and good will by:

  - Introducing people to others when there may be a good connection

  - Engaging "loners" in conversation

  - Providing directions (to the buffet table, restrooms), providing a pen or napkin, giving up your seat to another, etc.

Chapter 3 Reminders

The guidelines in this chapter will help you build solid professional relationships that will be valuable assets throughout your working life – and possibly beyond.

Review the reminders below. Check the ones you need to practice. Then continue to practice over the next weeks, months and years.

Section 1:

- ❒ Inventory your existing network.
- ❒ Identify places and organizations where you can meet professionals who may become part of your professional network.
- ❒ Repeat often throughout your working life.

Section 2: Give in return for what you get through networking

- ❒ Give back in the short term.
- ❒ Plan to give back in the long term – you never know when you may need to reach out to the other person or when you may be able to help others.
- ❒ Continuously follow up. If your contacts don't readily respond to email, call and leave a message.

Section 3: Go out to meet new people

- ❒ Prepare for events where you will meet professionals.
- ❒ Apply tips in this workbook for working a room.

CHAPTER 4

Powering Up Your Career Portfolio

A career portfolio is a collection of materials, both hard copy and electronic, that showcases your skills and attributes. It documents your educational accomplishments and your professional knowledge, skills, and experience. It is your marketing tool in selling yourself when you apply for internships, graduate school, and jobs.

Initially, your career portfolio will include your resume, bio, and references. As you develop in your profession, you'll add pertinent work samples, copies of honors and achievement awards, and recommendations of your abilities by others. Throughout your academic and working life, you'll need to periodically update your career portfolio so you're ready to apply for the next job or career opportunity.

You'll know your career portfolio is working for you when... you're encouraged to apply for positions and when you're invited for interviews.

Here are the most important parts of your career portfolio:

- Resume

- Professional bio

- References

- Photo

- Social media

- Your own online identity

- Cover letter

- Business cards

Resume Overview

1. Your resume

A resume is a document you create to present your education, skills, and background in a professional way. There is no one right or wrong way to develop a resume, and there are as many resume templates as there are resume reference books and websites. This chapter describes how to develop a resume that has proved effective for many college students. Your resume needs to be excellent because it is what is going to get you in the door for an interview. This chapter shows you how to achieve an excellent generic resume.

See examples in Chapter 5 for customizing your resume for a specific job.

The two main types of resume are ***"chronological"*** and ***"functional."***

The more commonly known ***chronological resume*** highlights employment history and lists company or organization name, position title, and dates of employment (most recent first), along with a brief description of associated job tasks and accomplishments. This type of resume is best suited for job seekers who have a fairly long history of consistent employment and promotions. Therefore the chronological resume will not be the focus in this workbook since most students don't have a list of increased responsibilities within many organizations.

The functional resume is a better choice for most students and recent graduates who lack a long history of work in their field. It highlights your assets and skills as well as the experience you have accumulated through a combination of education, work, and community involvement. The functional resume is also used by professionals who prefer to highlight and showcase their skills and accomplishments. There is also a hybrid resume that can combine the features of both chronological and functional resumes.

Within the functional resume category, there are some differences in treatment between general fields of study (e.g. liberal and creative arts, education, business, etc.) and the more technical (e.g. hard sciences, computer technology, medical research, etc.). These distinctions are clarified throughout this section.

Above the fold

The most important thing to remember about your resume is "above the fold" – the information that appears on the top third or half of the page. This is where you must capture immediate attention with your most outstanding characteristics, key words, and experience. It is the most valuable "real estate" because it's where recruiters and hiring managers spend the first 10 to 20 seconds deciding whether or not your application makes the cut.

A typical resume for a university student begins with the following sections:

- **Contact information.** Your full name, street address, email address, phone number, and, if you have one, your website address.

- **Education.** The name of your college or university, its location, area of study, major (double major or minor if you have one), when you expect to graduate, and overall GPA and/or GPA in your major (if you're particularly proud of it). If you are working while going to school, always include that with your GPA, e.g. "GPA 3.0 while working."

    Note: Education goes at the top if you are still in school. As soon as you graduate, the education section moves to the bottom. That's how recruiters can easily see your status for employment.

- **Highlights of Qualifications.** Bulleted list of the skills/qualifications/ expertise that set you apart from other candidates. Being fluent in multiple lanugagues and skilled with new technology should definitely be at the top! Be as specific as possible.

Poor: Strong communication skills

Better: Strong written and oral communications

Best: Editor for campus newspaper and skilled presenter

Other **Best statements:**

Excellent organizational skills proven by 3.7 GPA, while working 20 hours a week

Fluent in Spanish

Poor: Experience with latest technology

Better: Experience with Wordpress, HTML, InDesign and PhotoShop

Best: Proficiency and extensive experience using Wordpress, HTML, ...

The next "above the fold" sections vary depending on (a) whether your field is general or technical and (b) your strongest "selling points."

- **Relevant Coursework.** Specific courses that highlight your preparation. This is particularly valuable for those seeking opportunities in specialized areas of any profession like economics, psychology, computer science, etc.

- **Lab Experience.** (For technical fields) proficiency and experience with specific procedures, equipment and technology that highlight your qualifications.

- **Computer Skills.** This section is important, but do NOT put Word, Excel, email, internet, etc. That's like saying you know how to use a computer. Everyone expects that you know these. Definitely include specialized software (e.g., Photoshop, WordPress, HTML, website software and technologies, etc.).

Below the fold

- **Relevant Experience.** Expansion of the roles you have performed – both as employee and volunteer – including measurable results when possible. Always use headings and categories that are relevant for your experience and the job that you are applying. *Examples are:* Leadership, Supervision, Accounting, Writing and Editing.

- **Employment History.** Bulleted list of employers, your position, and dates of employment in chronological order, beginning with the most recent. List all your jobs, even those not associated with your field of study.

- **Relevant Community Experience.** (Optional) Bulleted list of the organizations, your role, and dates of participation, along with very brief descriptions of your roles.

- **Awards and Honors.** Limited to scholarships, academic awards and achievements, and community honors. Avoid acronyms unless you know reviewers will understand them.

The outline below displays one kind of template for a generic functional resume. *(See two examples of functional resumes at the end of this chapter.)*

YOUR NAME
Contact info: address, phone, email, website address

EDUCATION
List colleges and universities (most recent first), along with field(s) of study,
GPA (optional), expected graduation date.

HIGHLIGHTS OF QUALIFICATIONS
Short, bulleted statements about your most outstanding skills
(i.e., "Fluent in oral and written English and Spanish")

RELEVANT COURSEWORK (optional)
Specific classes relating to your field(s) of study

LAB EXPERIENCE (suggested for technical fields)
Specific proficiencies relating to the technical field(s) of study

- -(fold)- -

RELEVANT EXPERIENCE
Short, bulleted specifics about activities and responsibilities and, when possible,
measurable results

EMPLOYMENT HISTORY
(chronological list, most recent first)
Name of organization, your position
Dates of employment

RELEVANT COMMUNITY EXPERIENCE
(chronological list, most recent first)
Name of organization, your role
Dates of service
Under each organization, bulleted statements about the services you have contributed

AWARDS AND/OR HONORS
Academic and/or community awards, name of organization, and dates

---

Resume dos

- Keep your resume to one page unless you've had years of extensive work experience.

- Use strong action verbs throughout your resume and cover letter (see list of action verbs at the end of this chapter).

- In describing your experience, be specific. Use verbs such as "analyzed," "developed," and "negotiated." When possible, include results in measurable terms.

- Use common 11-point fonts such as Arial, Verdana, or Times. Your resume should be centered on the page. Change the margins so they work for you.

- Use all capitals, bold, and bullets to call attention to parts you want to emphasize. Do not use lines, which can interfere with formatting and databases on reviewers' systems.

- Ask several excellent writers to proofread your resume for errors and typos to ensure spelling and punctuation and especially grammar are 100% correct. You want your resume to look and read perfectly.

- Ask for feedback from your professional mentor and other professionals.

Resume don'ts

- Don't include an objective. This will narrow your options because hiring managers will think you are not open to other positions.

- Don't include common job tasks such as making copies or filing unless you're applying for a clerical position.

- Don't include names of references or even the phrase "References available on request." You will of course have to provide references. That is a given and takes up valuable space.

- Don't include personal information such as sports and hobbies unless they apply to your field of study or the position you're interested in.

- Don't include anything in your resume earlier than your freshman year in college. That includes high school GPA, employment, activities, honors, etc. Recruiters want to see only what you've done lately and in relation to your course of study and career goals.

- Don't rely on SpellCheck to find all the errors. It may miss words in context and does not report errors in words that are all caps (such as your headings).

- Don't use acronyms unless they are common language (e.g. "MS Word" is well-known as "Microsoft Word," whereas "PI" may have a number of meanings).

- Don't include anything that isn't true.

Remember: Your resume is never finished! Always update it as you gain experience, and always ask for another review and feedback from professional people.

2. Your references

As you get close to receiving an offer, the employer or program admissions officer will require several references. Your references will be professionals you know well enough to speak about your work ethic, integrity, honesty, and ability to get along with others. Do not use your friends or relatives.

Although you won't provide your references until requested, always ask your references' permission in advance. This boosts your credibility as a professional and allows your references to also be well prepared.

After you have provided the names and contact numbers, be sure to call your references to alert them. Provide your references with:

- The name of the institution and, if you know it, the name of the person who will be calling.

- Information about the kind of work or study that will be involved, so your references can prepare to discuss your skills, abilities, and attributes that apply to the position.

Once you know the outcome, always follow up with a thank you to the people who provided references – whether or not you were offered or accepted the position.

3. Your professional bio

This is created in addition to your resume. Your resume is a list of what you've done. Your bio is a narrative that focuses on your passion for your field of study, and where and how you want to use your knowledge and skills in a career. Your bio explains about the life experiences and ambition that are leading you to your career. It helps recruiters to learn about who you are.

Bios are:

- Sometimes requested by prospective employers.

- Always used in conjunction with – never instead of – your cover letter and resume.

- Useful additions to your LinkedIn and Visualcv.com profiles.

Bio dos

- Keep your bio to one page or less, and include a very good quality photo headshot.

- Write your bio using "he" or "she" (as if someone else has written it about you).

- Include goals and experiences that show growth and development in your academic and work experiences in your area of interest.

- Include special skills such as proficiency with other languages and perhaps how you've used them.

- In 3 to 4 sentences, tell why you are passionate about your chosen career.

- Ask several excellent writers to proofread your bio for errors and typos to make sure spelling, punctuation, and grammar are 100% correct.

- Ask for feedback from professionals.

Bio don'ts

- Don't write anything that does not portray you as professional.

- Don't write about old stories of your past or anything about family members, friends, or anyone but yourself.

- Don't write anything that isn't true.

There is no one-size-fits-all template for developing your bio. In fact, you may develop several different versions depending on how the bio will be used. The following activity will get you started, but do not be limited by it.

See examples of professional student bios on page 100.

ACTIVITY

Create your professional bio

Your full name _____
is a (freshman/sophomore/junior/senior/graduate student) at
(name of college or university) majoring in _____
and minoring in _____
[First name] has always been passionate about_____
_____
He/she is focused on using her knowledge and skills in the area
of _____
in order to_____

4. Your photo

There are times when a photo "headshot" is appropriate. Your portrait is an important marketing tool, and, as with other marketing tools, you need to use it strategically.

- Dress to reflect the norms of the profession that you hope to join. A shirt with collar is a good choice.

- Find a neutral, indoor background.

- Ask a friend to take your photo. You should have a relaxed, natural smile.

- Smile, and think positively so you will be communicating your energy, confidence, competency, and curiosity about the world.

- Stand up straight, shoulders back, with your body at an angle to the camera while facing forward (to avoid the "mug shot" look).

- Don't retouch the photo so much that meeting you in person is cause for mistrust.

- Don't include anything or anyone else in the photo.

- Use your photo on your LinkedIn, Visualcv.com, and other social media sites.

It's also a good idea to monitor other photos you're sharing online. Keeping in mind that your Facebook page, for example, can and will be viewed by others. Choose your photos carefully. Post only photos that relate to the professional image you are striving to convey. Clean up your Facebook page and visit it reguarly to see what others are seeing.

The same caution goes for photos that are posted and tagged by others. Be on the lookout for your photos that appear on friends' sites. Untag anything that you wouldn't want a decision maker to see.

5. Social media and websites for job searching

Although statistically face-to-face networking is the best way to make connections that lead to career opportunities, social media and the internet is extremely important too. It should be part of your marketing strategy. You can use online resources to identify people and positions, and when your credentials are online, employers can find you. LinkedIn, Google+ and Twitter gets the word out for you. Sites that list jobs and are often visited by recruiters include Monster.com, Craigslist.org, and OpportunityNOCS.org (for nonprofits), Indeed.com, Careerbuilder.com, usajobs.gov (the federal government official job site), and greenbiz.com (specifically for green jobs and careers). Remember to also visit your college career center's site for job listings.

LinkedIn

LinkedIn is designed for business professionals and business owners, not the general public. In fact, LinkedIn is so well established that in some circles a LinkedIn profile with connections is expected, even for undergraduates.

You establish yourself on LinkedIn by creating a professional profile. The text you include is searchable, so if you're looking for work in a particular area such as biology or public policy, be sure to add this information in your profile.

As with other social media sites, you then begin to ask people you know to become part of your LinkedIn network. LinkedIn is an effective way to find people with whom you've lost contact, and to make and strengthen new contacts by mutual sharing of information and referrals.

Here are a few ways to use LinkedIn:

- **LinkedIn Company Search** lets you access specific companies. If you find people in that organization who are connected to your personal contacts, you can ask your personal contact to introduce you.

- **LinkedIn Job Posting** allows employers to post jobs on the site. You can search for jobs that match your criteria.

- **LinkedIn Groups** are formed by individuals and organizations to focus on "special interests" and occupations. For example, if human resources is your focus, you can search and request to join LinkedIn Groups dedicated to topics and employment in that industry. Look for groups that not only have large numbers of members, but also those that show frequent activity. Read questions, and contribute to the online conversations. Initiate conversation by posting questions and information. This is a means of networking with other professionals in your field.

- **Email** – Let your connections know when you are looking for work and what type you are looking for by sending email. Ask for help and referrals and connections to people they know.

LinkedIn dos

- Educate yourself about the features of LinkedIn.

- Fill out the profile as completely as possible, including your professional-quality headshot.

- Make sure that everything you post portrays you as professional.

- Ask an excellent writer to review your profile information.

- Join LinkedIn groups and participate actively.

- Update your information as your job search and professional accomplishments change (your LinkedIn connections automatically receive updates).

LinkedIn don'ts

- Don't send mass invitations. Personalize each one with a message you compose.

Google+

Creating pages and professional contacts, separate from your friends, is always a good addition to your networking.

Facebook

While Facebook is most commonly used to connect friends for social purposes, it can also be an effective professional networking and job search tool. You can create groups and join other common-interest user groups, organized by workplace, school or college, or other characteristics.

- Post status updates that let people know you're looking. Mention, for example, that you made a great contact at a networking event.

Facebook dos

- Remember that recruiters and hiring managers can (and do) access Facebook pages for information. Whatever you post may be viewable. Always check your pictures and comments.

- Avoid posting or responding to controversial comments (e.g. political or religious views) that might discourage consideration of your professional qualities.

6. Your own online identity

In addition to establishing yourself online with social media, you can create a searchable identity using a variety of online applications. The following sites are a short list of possibilities.

What	Why	How
Create your own website	Distinguish yourself from other job seekers by highlighting your skills, abilities, and talents and by telling your own story.	Use free website creation software such as www.moonfruit.com, www.google.com/placesforbusiness, or www.weebly.com Some offer free hosting.
Blog	Create useful, topical content and insight into your professional field of expertise. Respond to the blogs of others who share your career focus and vision.	Use free blog creation software such as www.google.com/blogger, www.wordpress.com, or www.convozine.com
Post your resume	Provide employers with another way to find you.	Post your resume on sites such as www.VisualCV.com and www.Monster.com

Chapter 4 Reminders

Keep your career portfolio current and ready for the next opportunity. Remember to add any new skills or experience. Always edit, edit and edit!

Section 1: Your resume

- ❏ Develop a generic functional resume that is perfect and ready to customize.
- ❏ Carefully plan "above the fold" information to highlight your most important and distinguishing characteristics, skills and experiences.
- ❏ Use action verbs to describe your relevant experience.
- ❏ Ask professionals to review and offer suggestions.
- ❏ Ask an excellent writer to proof read your resume so it stands the best chance of being 100% free of grammatical, spelling, or punctuation errors.

Section 2: Your references

- ❏ Ask professionals in your network in advance for the favor of providing references.
- ❏ When you have provided references' names to prospects, call your references with a "heads up" that they may be contacted.
- ❏ Whether or not your application results in the position you want, thank your references and let them know the results.

Section 3: Your professional bio

- ❏ Develop a professional bio that includes your photo.
- ❏ Limit your bio to about a half a page, no more than a page.
- ❏ Ask a professional to review it and offer suggestions.
- ❏ Ask an excellent writer to proofread it so it stands the best chance of being 100% free of grammatical, spelling, or punctuation errors.

Section 4: Your photo

☐ Your image is extremely important. Obtain a quality head shot for use in bios, social media profiles, and websites.

☐ Be strategic about photos of you that appear online, on both your social media sites and friends' sites. Remove or untag photos that do not portray you in a professional way.

Section 5: Social media

☐ Join LinkedIn, complete the profile, and keep it up to date.

☐ Ask contacts to connect with you, inviting them with personalized messages.

☐ Join LinkedIn and Google+ professional groups, and become actively involved.

☐ Use Facebook and other social media sites strategically.

Section 6: Your own online identity

☐ Show your entrepreneurial qualities by creating your own website.

☐ Post your resume on websites such as Monster.com and VisualCV.com.

☐ Consider a blog and/or contribute to the blogs of others who share your career focus and vision.

Action Verbs for Resumes and Cover Letters

Use strong verbs such as these to indicate your employable skills

Management	Technical	Creative
Analyzed	Assembled	Conceptualized
Attained	Built	Created
Chaired	Calculated	Customized
Contracted	Computed	Designed
Coordinated	Designed	Developed
Developed	Engineered	Established
Evaluated	Operated	Illustrated
Improved	Programmed	Initiated
Increased	Remodeled	Invented
Organized	Repaired	Originated
Planned	Solved	Performed
Strengthened	Upgraded	Revitalized
Supervised		

Supervised	Teaching	Helping
Communication	Adapted	Assessed
Addressed	Advised	Assisted
Arbitrated/mediated	Clarified	Clarified
Authored	Coached	Coached
Convinced	Communicated	Collaborated
Developed	Delivered	Demonstrated
Drafted	Developed	Diagnosed
Formulated	Enabled	Educated
Negotiated	Evaluated	Expedited
Publicized	Facilitated	Guided
Spoke	Guided	Motivated
Translated	Instructed	Rehabilitated
Wrote	Trained	Represented

Research	Financial	Detail oriented
Clarified	Allocated	Approved
Critiqued	Analyzed	Catalogued
Diagnosed	Appraised	Classified
Evaluated	Audited	Executed
Inspected	Budgeted	Generated
Interpreted	Calculated	Implemented
Organized	Computed	Monitored
Summarized	Forecasted	Organized
Surveyed	Projected	Prepared
Systematized	Researched	Systematized
		Validated

Example Functional Resume – *General Field of Study*

Robin Robine

213 Willow Street Anytown, Anystate 80111
Robin.Robine@gmail.com Cell phone: 999-999-9999 www.RobinRobine.net

EDUCATION
- University of Your State (UYS), Springfield
- Expected graduation December 2014
- Major: Business Administration Minor: Education
- Cumulative 3.2 GPA while working

HIGHLIGHTS OF QUALIFICATIONS
- Effective leader with ability to prioritize, delegate, and motivate
- Experienced in collaborating with others on group projects, as both leader and contributor
- Experienced Spanish translator, both oral and written
- Power user of MS Office Pro 2010 (Excel, Access, OneNote, Publisher, Visio)

RELEVANT COURSEWORK
- Macro and Micro Economics, Calculus, Statistics, Foundations of Education, Cognitive Psychology

RELEVANT EXPERIENCE
PROGRAM PLANNING & COORDINATING
- Collaborated with after-school teen program advisors and directors to establish and implement programs that were accepted by teen participants
- Development and delivery of four teen mentoring programs that became the model for three community centers
- Recruited and trained teens in peer mentoring techniques that resulted in 50% increase in retention and participation in the program
- Developed and delivered bilingual financial education program for non-English speakers, specifically addressing the concept and importance of saving and investing

NEEDS ASSESSMENT/ADVISING
- Administered and allocated funds for the teen counseling program, managing funds within budget
- Initiated investigation into the need for bullying prevention program and presented a report to school administrators
- Conducted bilingual survey, analyzed the results, and reported finding to program directors

EMPLOYMENT HISTORY
Aug. 2012 - Current Peer Advisor Student Service Program
Jun. 2012 - Oct. 2012 Security Monitor Summer Bridge
May 2011 - Jun. 2011 Civic Engagement Canvasser InnerCity Struggle
Mar. 2011 - Jun. 2011 Tutor/High School Counselor/Upward Bound

RELEVANT COMMUNITY AND VOLUNTEER EXPERIENCE
Jan. 2012 Philanthropy Chair, Pi Lambda Phi (Academic Fraternity)
Sept. 2011 Service Director, Springfield Community Center
Sept. 2011 Outreach Committee Member, Springfield Community Center
Jan. 2012 Extern at Children's Aid Society, Mytown, NX
Sept. 2011 Bilingual Tutor, XYZ Hall on campus
Sept. 2011 - May 2013 Co-President, Tingle Hall on campus

AWARDS and HONORS
- Recipient of full scholarship, ABC Scholarship Fund
- Recipient of 14th District Political Scholarship
- GHK Leadership Program - outstanding academic achievements and leadership awards
- Outstanding Volunteer of the Year 2010, Springfield Community Center

Example Functional Resume – *Technical Field of Study*

Francis Remi Cappa

3211 Oak Street Apt. 721 Anytown, Anystate 80111
FRCappa@xmail.net Cell phone: 999-999-9999

EDUCATION
- San Francisco State, Intended graduation: May 20yy
- Major: Molecular Environmental Biology – Human Health
- Minor: Molecular Toxicology

HIGHLIGHTS OF QUALIFICATIONS
- **Scientific research:** Planned and executed a study of the effect of caffeine on sleep disorders
- **Leadership:** Developed and delivered a program to build teen awareness of the hazards of recreational prescription drug use
- **Communication:** Tutored first-year biology and chemistry students in principles and lab techniques

RELEVANT COURSEWORK
- Organic Chemistry, Biology, Biochemistry, Genetics, Physiology, Endocrinology, Microbiology

LAB SKILLS
- Proficiency with ToTheMax microplate reader, Incubation, Centrifugation, Thin Layer Photography, MoleculareBioProfile 1011.0 software

RELEVANT EXPERIENCE
- Conducted in vitro experiments using test animal microsomes
- Performed sensitivity studies to quantitatively examine effects of common pharmaceuticals
- Analyzed the metabolism of substrates of the AAA enzyme to determine addictive effects
- Evaluated DNA samples to determine causes of degeneration
- Gathered proper samples in field research and demonstrated how to use dissecting instruments

EMPLOYMENT HISTORY
GoTo Pharmaceuticals, Inc., Research internship, *Dec. 2012 – Present*
Merrydale Marine Labs, Inc., Research Internship, Merrydale, NX, *May-July 2011*

RELEVANT COMMUNITY AND VOLUNTEER EXPERIENCE
Downtown Free Clinic, Lab Volunteer, *June 2012 – Present*
- Laboratory skills: microscope techniques and gram staining
- Other tasks: intake, data entry, quality assurance reading for samples sent for further testing

Teen-time Community House, Peer Advisor, *September 2011 – Present*
- Mentored science majors regarding classes, research opportunities, etc.

Ageless Health, Volunteer, *October 2011 – May 2012*
- Maintained email accounts, listserves, websites, promoted organization events
- Organized club socials and fundraisers

Diabetes Awareness Project, Volunteer Trainer, *September 2011 – May 2012*
- Delivered workshops at downtown high schools for 30-40 students per session
- Educated teens on the biology, early detection, and preventative steps

Professional bio examples

Robin Robine

Robin Robine is a senior at the University of Your State (UYS) majoring in Business Administration with a minor in Education. Her expected graduation date is December 2013.

Robin's interests and academic successes have fueled her passion for community service. While her persistence and excellent academic record have earned her numerous awards and scholarships, her volunteer endeavors have provided her with the opportunity to take leading roles in non-profit organizations.

As a student she has excelled working with both adults and children. In her work as Service Director at the Springfield Community Center, she organized and coached adult volunteers. As Outreach Committee member, she helped acquire major corporate donors.

Robin's knowledge and preparation have positioned her as an invaluable resource to community service organizations. Robin is preparing to carry out her commitment to service with a career in the non-profit sector.

Francis Remi Cappa

Francis Remi Cappa is a junior at San Francisco State. With a major in Biology and a minor in Molecular Toxicology, Francis intends to graduate in May 2014.

Francis has always been passionate about helping others. He demonstrates strong leadership in academics, employment, and community service.

As a student, he excels at lab subjects while tutoring others. As an intern for GoTo Labs, he planned and executed a study on the effects of caffeine on sleep disorders. The results became the subject of a white paper that appears on the company's web site.

As a concerned citizen, Francis has developed a program to educate teens about the dangers inherent in the recreational use of prescription drugs, and as his schedule permits, he personally delivers the program to local junior high and high schools.

Following graduation from San Francisco State, Francis plans on working in the pharmaceutical field for a time before enrolling in a school of medicine and ultimately earning a degree leading him to a career goal of becoming a general practitioner.

CHAPTER 5

Creating Your Job Search Strategy

You'll increase the odds of success when you approach your job search as an entrepreneur. That means developing a vision of the career you want, gathering information and marketing effectively, and taking meticulous care with your applications, interviewing and negotiating.

In this chapter, you build on the great work you've already completed. Now you're ready to identify and apply for opportunities in your field.

You'll know you're successful when ... you are locating the right opportunities and you are being called for interviews.

The actions are:

- Schedule informational interviews.

- Research job openings.

- Apply for openings with a strategic and structured approach.

- Look for specifics in the job posting.

- Customize your generic resume to the job posting.

- Create a compelling cover letter.

- Make your application and delivery stand out from others

I. Engage in informational interviews

An informational interview is not a job interview. It is a pre-arranged meeting with a professional who is employed in a field you're interested in pursuing. During the interview, you gather valuable, first-hand information about a career field or industry, a specific job within the field, and/or a specific organization. Informational interviews differ from job interviews in these ways:

- You request the interview and take charge by leading the discussion and asking most of the questions.

- There is no position opening (or at least one you know about).

- You shouldn't appear to be looking for a job at the organization.

How to obtain informational interviews

There are several ways informational interviews can be arranged:

- As you build rapport with professionals, ask if they would be willing to help you gather career/job/company information by talking with you at some agreed-upon day and time. Fifteen to thirty minutes is sufficient and usually causes the least disruption to busy professionals.

- Review your Professional Network Contact List (see Chapter 3) and check with your college career center. Call or individually email people who may have connections in your field. Ask for introductions to professionals. When you first make contact, mention the name of the person who introduced you.

Face-to-face informational interviews are preferred, but telephone interviews can work well, too, and they're often easier to arrange.

Note: When asking a person in your network to help you obtain an informational interview, ask for an "introduction" rather than a "referral."

When requesting an interview by email or phone, you can use this as a template:

Dear Mr./Ms. Smith:

I am a _____ [year in school] majoring in _____ at _____ [name of your school]. We talked briefly at _____ [name of event, date, place]

-OR-

I heard you speak at _____ [name of event, date, place]

-OR-

_____ [name of contact] suggested I get in touch with you.

I'm interested in learning all I can about the [specific name of] profession/field of work.

Would you be so kind as to give me 15 to 30 minutes of your time in the next 2 weeks to meet and answer some of my questions about your role as [position] in the field?

Thank you for your consideration. I will contact you next week to follow up, or please contact me in the meantime at this email address or my cell phone: 230-999-9999.

Thank you,

How to prepare for and conduct informational interviews

In preparation for an informational interview:

- Prepare a list of questions that address your curiosity about the industry or field, the job, the organization, and the person you're interviewing.

- If the meeting is face-to-face, dress professionally.

- Whether face-to-face or by phone, be prepared to use all your best relationship-building skills. See Chapter 6 for more tips about interviewing.

- Always arrive or call on time.

Suggested questions to ask during the informational interview

Following are some typical (but not all-inclusive) questions. It's okay to bring your list of questions to an interview. It shows you're prepared. Tailor them to the situation.

- What was the path that led you to this field and job?

- What do you most enjoy about your work?

- What, if any, are your frustrations?

- What is the secret of success in this industry/field?

- What is the future of this industry/field?

- What are the educational requirements? What other training is recommended?

- What internship and/or work experience is generally expected?

- What, if any, outside activities or experiences are expected or helpful?

- What's the best way to break into this field?

- What are the hard skills employers in this field generally seek?

- What are opportunities for advancement?

- Which skills are most important to acquire?

- What are the employment prospects in this industry/field? Geographically, where are the best employment prospects?

- What are some related occupations?

- What are the different salary ranges?

- Is this industry/field growing? Shrinking? How rapidly?

- What's the best way to find open positions?

- What do you know now that you wish you'd known when you entered this field?

- What else should I know that I haven't asked about the industry/field or job?

- Are there other people in the field/industry I should be talking with? Can you make an introduction?

- If I have additional questions that we didn't cover this time, may I call you?

Following the interview:

- Send a thank you to the person you interviewed. Tell at least one specific thing that was most helpful (e.g., I especially appreciate your insight into ... I had not realized .... That will be helpful to me in ...)

- If you obtained the interview through an introduction, also send a thank you to the person who referred you.

- When you are settled in a job, send another thank you to the person along with your contact information. Email is appropriate for this message, but a hand-written note is a nicer touch and allows you to enclose your new business card.

- If you obtained the interview through an introduction, send a similar thank you to the person who made the introduction.

- Refer back to Chapter 3 for additional relationship building follow-up activities.

2. Research job openings

According to many career professionals, at least 75% of jobs are found via networking. That means that 75% of your time should be spent networking. The remainder can be spent researching job openings in other ways. The table below provides some useful websites.

Website	Description
www.LinkedIn.com	This social networking site is used primarily by professionals to find and maintain contacts and to job search. It is free to join and offers limited free job searches.
www.Monster.com	This is a free database of position openings. Enter location and job title. The site also includes helpful career and job search tips and guidelines.
www.Indeed.com	This free database of position openings is assembled from organizations' websites and some employer-paid posts. No registration is required. Enter the zip code and a job title. You can also request listings matching your criteria to be sent directly to your email inbox.
www.TheLadders.com	Search available jobs, and review job search tips. Subscription is required. A free subscription allows you to view job titles only. Paying subscribers have unlimited access to the job database.
www.CareerBuilder.com	In addition to free job search (by position name and geographic location), there is a wealth of how-to job search information.
www.Idealist.org www.opportunityknocks.org	Visit these sites for job opportunities in non-profit organizations.

Be sure to keep checking your university's job postings site.

3. Apply for job openings with a strategic and structured approach

As you begin identifying jobs that match your education and skill levels, use your time wisely by applying for jobs ONLY when there's a good match. By carefully analyzing the specifics of the job posting and researching the organization's mission, you'll have a good idea about whether you want and/or have a reasonable chance of getting a posted position.

However you discover job openings, the following three steps are essential:

- Look for specifics in the job posting.

- Customize your resume matching the job posting with your skills and experience with the stated requirements.

- Create a compelling cover letter.

4. Look for specifics in the job posting

The resume you send in response to an open position may be one of hundreds, and the initial reviewer may be an electronic scanner. Whether by scanner or human, the first pass will screen for key words that exactly match the job posting.

That means no matter how well written your generic resume (see Chapter 4), you must customize it to include the right key words and qualifications – both above and below the fold.

Steps in analyzing the job posting

Find and note the key words and phrases that pertain to education, knowledge, skills, and experience.

1. **Review the job posting:**

   - **Education.** Look for degree requirements. Some job postings specify "X degree or equivalent experience." If you do not have the exact degree(s), you will need to demonstrate extensive work experience as an alternative.

   - **Job requirements.** Look for and circle "hard" skills and knowledge such as technology, research, writing and editing, language fluency, etc. Job requirements usually are prefaced by words such as "minimum, "preferred," "essential," "significant," "demonstrated," "desirable," "a plus," "the ideal candidate will ..." etc.

   Note: In contrast, terms such as "team player," "intuitive," "creative," or "self-starter" are "soft" skills. These typically do not belong above the fold unless the job posting precedes them with words such as "mandatory," or "must have." Otherwise, soft skills can be woven into the "Relevant Experience" section of the resume and/or the cover letter.

   - **Job responsibilities.** Look for and underline phrases such as "Primary duties include ...," and "Must be able to ...," etc.

2. **Create a table with a list of job requirements and responsibilities in the left column, matched with your skills and experience on the right.**

Job posting requirements and responsibilities	My skills and experience that match

While job postings frequently specify every possible skill and experience possibly needed, employers do not necessarily expect to find them all in one candidate. Therefore, if your qualifications appear to be a reasonable match, continue with the application. Some skills and experience, such as selling and project management, may be transferable from one field to another.

5. Customize your generic resume to the job posting

The key words indicating your skills, abilities, and experiences must match the job posting, and they must be easy for the scanner or reviewer to find. In addition, everything must be true.

Above the fold

Highlights of Qualifications

- Develop maximum five standout sentences that correspond to the job posting.

- Where possible, use the exact key words.

- List your qualifications in rank order of importance to the job responsibilities and requirements.

- Delete anything that doesn't correspond to the job posting.

Relevant Coursework (optional)

- Retain courses relevant to the job posting.

- Omit courses that are not relevant.

Below the fold

Relevant Experience

- Use action verbs such as "delivered," "produced," "led," "organized," etc. to showcase your skills, abilities, and experience. (See Chapter 5, Action Verbs.)

- When possible, describe measurable results that showcase your achievements (*Examples:* "increased by 20%," or "received top award for ...").

- Omit experiences that do not apply.

Community or Volunteer Experience

- Include experiences that showcase the "soft" skills that are specified in the job posting. Examples are self-starter, motivated, great communication skills.

As you finish customizing your resume, continue asking yourself if this job fits your vision of your career and your next job. If you are successful in getting the interview, you will learn things about the organization – positive or negative – that did not come through the job posting.

No matter how attached you are to some of your achievements, such as irrelevant education, skills, and experience; including these indicates you do not fully understand the needs of the job. They also take up valuable space needed for important viable information for the position.

Activity 5-1: Review the customized resume for Robin Robine

At the end of this chapter, there is a sample job posting, generic resume, and customized resume.

1. Review the job posting for education requirements, job requirements, and job responsibilities.

2. Review Robin's generic resume (page 128). Answer the question: "Does Robin need to customize this resume?" If yes, consider what changes she should make.

3. Review Robin's customized resume (page 127). Notice how she has changed the sections above the fold to include key words. Compare generic and customized versions below the fold.

6. Create a compelling cover letter

A cover letter typically accompanies every resume or application. The purpose is to complement your resume by adding a personal touch and an initial positive impression. There are two styles of professional cover letters. One is called the executive summary, the other is a traditional cover letter. It can make the difference between being invited for an interview – or not. People who are hiring want to be sure you have professional writing skills, and that you understand the format and style of a professional letter.

A well-developed cover letter:

- Demonstrates you understand the requirements of the position.

- Demonstrates clear and concise writing skills.

- Is limited to one page (Keep sentences short, and limit paragraphs to 3-4 sentences).

- Addresses the most important requirements and responsibilities using key words.

- Focuses on the employer's needs, not yours. Recruiters see too many letters focusing on why the candidate wants the job rather than what the candidate can do for the organization or bring to the position.

- Is 100% grammatically correct, with perfect spelling and punctuation.

Develop a connection to the organization

Knowledge, skills, and experience aside, employers hire people who appear to be a good fit for the organization and with whom they feel a positive connection.

Telling a brief "story" about why your background and/or passion for the work connects to the organization's mission will help you stand out from other candidates. Stories are memorable and repeatable. They provide insight about your character and charisma. Remember this must be relative to the position and why you would be a good candidate.

Activity 5-2: Create a compelling story about your connection to the mission of the organization

As part of your cover letter, do the following.

1. Research the mission of the organization. The website should provide important information if not an outright statement.

2. Identify something specific in your background (academic studies, work experience, or life) that shows a strong interest and/or commitment to the organization's mission.

3. Compose a 2- to 4-sentence brief "story" about your connection to the mission of the organization.

    *   *Example:* If you are applying for a position that requires interaction with disadvantaged people, consider a brief story such as:

        My first internship was in the Center for the Blind. I soon knew that this is what I want as my career because I immediately had a connection with the work, staff and clients. I got enormous satisfaction from my hard work, and I was very grateful for the opportunity.

Now you're ready to compose your cover letter. The following are examples of the executive summary and the traditional cover letter.

Executive Summary Cover Letter Example

Robin Robine
213 Willow Street Anytown, Anystate 80111
Robin.Robine@gmail.com Cell phone: 999-999-9999 www.RobinRobine.net

January 5, 2015

Ms. Sarah Smith-Jones
Assistant Director of Youth Programs
Springfield Museum
Albany, California 94706

Dear Ms. Smith-Jones:

I am a graduating senior at the University of California, Santa Cruz, majoring in Business Administration and minoring in Education. I am submitting my application for the position of Teen Docent Manager at the Springfield Museum. My major and my experience with developing and delivering teen programs, will give me the opportunity to make an important contribution to the museum and its patrons.

I believe the skills, qualities, and experience you seek are well matched by my record of accomplishments:

Your Needs	My Qualifications
Experience in program planning and coordination	· Planned, coordinated, and delivered program in bilingual financial education for non-English speakers
Proficiency in developing and delivering teen programming	· Developed educational programs for teen mentors and financial education for non-English speakers
	· Planned and coordinated delivery of four teen mentoring programs that became the model for three community centers
Highly developed analytical and reporting skills	· Conducted bilingual research project, analyzed results, and reported findings
Recruitment of teens and team management	· Recruited and trained teens in peer mentoring techniques, resulting in 50% increase in retention and participation in the program

Your mission of creating educational outreach and finding new and innovative ways to engage and inspire the public especially resonates with me because some of my fondest memories are the times I have spent in the Springfield Museum, viewing and learning from the exhibits, and doing research for school assignments. In my interactions with teens, I have learned the importance of gaining buy-in through incorporating their involvement. My passion for developing young people, plus my own love of learning have led me to apply for this position. I hope to have the opportunity to meet you in person to further discuss how my qualifications and focus match the needs of the Springfield Museum.

Thank you for your time and consideration.

Sincerely,

Robin Robine

Note: Exact wording from position description

Specifics that address each need

Compelling story about the connection to the organization's mission

Traditional Cover Letter Example

Jason Smith
457 Oak Drive
Smithtown, New York 11787
631-290-4756
jason.smith@gmail.com

October 27, 2012

Ms. Susan Ramer
Director, Human Resources
Capitol Recording
1440 Parker Street
East Islip, NY 11730

Dear Ms. Ramer:

I am a junior majoring in Psychology and Public Relations with a minor in Music at Hofstra University. I am responding to the position as Public Relations Intern that was recently posted on monster.com. I believe my studies along with my experience, passion for music and the recording industry make me a strong candidate for this position.

In my role as copywriter for the weekly university newspaper, I work with the editorial staff to deliver features that appeal to the student body. Thriving in a fast-paced team environment, I research and pitch stories that frequently rate front-page coverage. I also edit the popular "Music Matters" column. As a contributor to the overall publication process, I often fill in as copyeditor and proofreader as needed, making sure that our paper is on-time and of the highest editorial quality. Last summer I interned with Pine Communications, a local PR agency that specializes in social media and web promotions. In that role, I learned the basics of public relations, in addition to how to write press releases and media alerts.

Your mission of discovering, developing, and marketing recording artists is particularly intriguing to me. I have always had a passion for music and the recording industry. In my classes at Hofstra University, I am in regular contact with talented young musicians who plan to make music their careers. Upon graduation, my hope is to help musicians like them realize their dreams.

Thank you for taking the time to review my letter and attached resume. I look forward to speaking with you and discussing how my skills and abilities closely match the needs of Capitol Recording.

Sincerely,

(your signature)

Jason Smith

Cover Letter Guidelines

Heading (same as at the top of your resume)

Current Date

Name of Contact
Title of Contact
Name of Company
Address

Dear Ms._____ or Mr._____ :

(Try not to write the very overused To whom it may concern – very old school!)

If you can't find out the contact's name use "Dear Members of the Selection Committee."

FIRST PARAGRAPH

Make your first sentence stand out. Identify the position name and (if applicable) the position number. Then grab attention with a statement about why you are a good fit for the position.

Example:

> I am a graduating senior majoring in [your major] at [name of college or university], I am submitting my application for [exact name and number of the position]. I believe my experience with _____ along with my recent studies in _____ make me a strong candidate for this position.

If you were referred to the position by someone known to an employee of the organization or a member of the selection committee, begin with that information.

Example:

[Name of referrer] suggested I contact you. As a graduating senior majoring in ...

THE "EXECUTIVE SUMMARY" SECTION – a way to showcase your skills as they relate to job requirements

In this section, you create a two-column table with the headings "Your Needs" and "My Qualifications." In the left column, list the 4 to 5 primary job requirements and responsibilities as identified from the table you created in this chapter. Use the exact key words from the job posting. In the right column, list your qualifications and experience that address those needs.

Example:

Your Needs	My Qualifications
Analytical skills and judgment	Ran analytical assays for characterizing protein stability, analyzing data, and presenting results verbally and in reports
Clinical lab experience using specialized software	Used automated liquid handling systems and robotic systems. Analyzed data and reported results using microplate reader, incubation, centrifugation, and thin layer photography
Leadership	Developed and delivered a program to build community awareness of the hazards of recreational prescription drug use
Strong communication skills	Tutored first-year biology and chemistry students in principles and lab techniques

FINAL PARAGRAPHS (CLOSING)

- Make one last strong statement about why you are a great fit. Tell why you are excited about this position and how this organization's mission and goals align with your values and experience. You might want to use some of the same wording from your professional bio (see Chapter 4).

- Thank the reader for taking the time to review your cover letter and resume.

- Sincerely

Example:

Your mission of bringing life-saving products to market especially resonates with me. Modern medicines have been instrumental in lengthening and improving the quality of life for several members of my family. I am committed to applying my knowledge and skills and my highest level of commitment to the job of Research Analyst at ABC Pharma.

I hope to have the opportunity to meet you in person to further discuss how my qualifications and focus match the needs of ABC Pharma and how I can best help in achieving your mission.

Thank you for your time and consideration.

Sincerely,

Name

Activity 5-3: Review the Robin Robine cover letter

Study Robin's cover letter as it relates to:

- Key words from the job posting

- Key words in Robin's revised resume

- The connection between her background and the mission of the organization

7. The final step to submitting your application

Your application is almost ready. There are two more critical steps: **Proofread and follow through after you send.**

Proofread

As with all your professional correspondence, everything you create must be perfect. Before pressing "Send," follow this proofreading checklist for your resume, bio and cover letter.

- Re-read both resume and cover letter 2 or 3 times, at least one time out loud.

- Use spellcheck (but don't totally rely on it).

- Check punctuation (especially commas and capitalization).

- Ask an excellent proofreader to verify that grammar is correct.

- Ensure that the font is consistent throughout (including size).

- Be sure your letter is centered on the paper and looks perfect.

- Edit and proof again.

Put both cover letter and resume into the same PDF document to ensure that they stay together, they are readable by different versions of software, and that the formatting will not change.

Create a cover email for the PDF attachment. Include the exact name (and job number if applicable) in the email cover. Make the email subject line stand out with a statement such as "Strong match for [position name and position number]." When sending an electronic resume, always save it with your name such as JoeSmith.doc or SandraHernandez.pdf. Never save the file as Resume21.doc. You want your resume to be easily identifiable and retrievable.

Exception: Some applications must be submitted online using the organization's template form, with no opportunity to attach a cover letter. In such cases, when there is an optional Comments box, use the space to make a compelling statement such as "Strong match for [position name and number]."

Follow through

Most job applicants email the cover letter and resume and then wait for a response. If you know the name and contact information of the organization, in addition to sending the email within two days, call to ensure that your email was received.

Chapter 5 Reminders

Section 1: Engage in Informational Interviews

☐ Ask professionals for informational interviews.

☐ Prepare questions in advance.

☐ Apply your best relationship building skills before, during, and after the interview.

☐ Follow up with thank you notes to interviewees and referrers.

Section 2: Research job openings

☐ Use your professional network to find open positions.

☐ Research opportunities in key internet sites and your college career center.

Section 3: Apply for openings with a strategic and structured approach

☐ Apply for positions only when you find a good match between the job and your knowledge, skills, and abilities.

☐ Use a structured approach to applying in order to maximize the opportunity.

Section 4: Look for specifics in the job posting

☐ Identify key words that signify the "hard skills" relating to job requirements and job responsibilities.

☐ Create a table of job requirements and responsibilities matched to your qualifications.

Section 5: Customize your resume to the job posting

- ❒ Edit your generic resume to incorporate exact key words from the job posting.
- ❒ In the Highlights of Qualifications section, list key skills in order of the job posting priority.
- ❒ Edit the resume "below the fold" to include key words where possible.
- ❒ Eliminate knowledge and skills that are not listed or alluded to in the job posting.

Section 6: Create a compelling cover letter

- ❒ Create a persuasive first paragraph.
- ❒ Consider creating an **Executive Summary** cover letter with a "Your Needs" and "My Qualifications" table with four to five key job responsibilities and requirements.
- ❒ Create a connection between you and the organization's mission.

Section 7: Make your application and delivery stand out from others

- ❒ Carefully proof read your resume and cover letter.
- ❒ (When possible) within a couple of days following the submission, call to check that the application was received.

8. Job Posting Example

Position Description: Teen Docent Manager

The Springfield Museum is committed to leading-edge research, educational outreach, and finding new and innovative ways to engage and inspire the public.

This position reports to the Assistant Director of Youth Programs for the Springfield Museum. The Teen Docent Manager is responsible for the development, delivery, and enhancement of the Museum's new Teen Docent Program. Through this program, Springfield youth (8th through 12th graders) will receive docent training, enabling them to help develop and deliver public programs and products for all ages of Museum visitors.

The ideal candidate will possess a combination of the following education and/or equivalent experiences:

- Bachelors or Masters degree in business and/or education
- Experience in program planning and coordination required
- Proficiency in developing and delivering teen programming in an informal environment, including training youth as public educators
- Highly developed analytical skills, along with the ability to create and conduct research projects, then analyze and report results

ESSENTIAL DUTIES AND RESPONSIBILITIES:

In collaboration with the Assistant Director of Youth Programs and other appropriate staff, the primary duties include developing, piloting, and launching the Teen Docent Program. Tasks will include but not be limited to:

- Develop educational programs for teens to use in public education, incorporating youth involvement as appropriate
- Create youth experiences that enhance Museum visitor experiences through interactions with program participants
- Actively cultivate teens through recruitment, ongoing training, team building, and recognition
- Oversee the Teen Docent Program budget and evaluation, and help with preparations of reports and proposals as requested
- Actively promote the Teen Docent Program and the Teacher & Youth Education Department internally and externally
- Collaborate with Education and other Museum staff on programmatic initiatives
- Successful candidate must be a self-starter, solid team player, and enthusiastic supporter of the Museum, both internally and within the community at large.

Customized Resume to job description

Robin Robine

213 Willow Street Anytown, Anystate 80111
Robin.Robine@gmail.com Cell phone: 999-999-9999 www.RobinRobine.net

EDUCATION
* University of Your State (UYS), Springfield
* Expected graduation December 2014
* Major: Business Administration Minor: Education
* Cumulative 3.2 GPA while working

HIGHLIGHTS OF QUALIFICATIONS
* Planned and coordinated financial education programs for non-English speakers
* Developed and delivered teen programs that involved the teens as mentors to others
* Created and conducted research for a bilingual research project, analyzed and reported the results
* Cultivated teens through recruitment, training, and teambuilding

RELEVANT COURSEWORK
* Macro and Micro Economics, Calculus, Statistics, Foundations of Education, Cognitive Psychology

RELEVANT EXPERIENCE
PROGRAM PLANNING & COORDINATING
* Collaborated with after-school teen program advisors and directors to establish and implement programs that were accepted by teen participants
* Planned, coordinated, and delivered four teen mentoring programs that became the model for three community centers
* Planned and coordinated bilingual financial education program for non-English speakers, specifically addressing the concept and importance of saving and investing
* Recruited and trained teens in teambuilding and peer mentoring techniques that resulted in 50% increase in retention and participation in the program

NEEDS ASSESSMENT/ADVISING
* Created and conducted bilingual research project, analyzed the results, and reported finding to program directors
* Initiated investigation into the need for bullying prevention program and presented a report to school administrators
* Oversaw and allocated funds for the teen counseling program, managing funds within budget

EMPLOYMENT HISTORY
Aug. 2012 - Current Peer Advisor Student Service Program
Jun. 2012 - Oct. 2012 Security Monitor Summer Bridge
May 2011 - Jun. 2011 Civic Engagement Canvasser InnerCity Struggle
Mar. 2011 - Jun. 2011 Tutor/High School Counselor/Upward Bound

RELEVANT COMMUNITY AND VOLUNTEER EXPERIENCE
Jan. 2012   Philanthropy Chair, Pi Lambda Phi (Academic Fraternity)
Sept. 2011 Service Director, Springfield Community Center
Sept. 2011 Outreach Committee Member, Springfield Community Center
Jan. 2012   Extern at Children's Aid Society, Mytown, NX
Sept. 2011 Bilingual Tutor, XYZ Hall on campus
Sept. 2011 - May 2013 Co-President, Tingle Hall on campus

AWARDS and HONORS
* Recipient of full scholarship, ABC Scholarship Fund
* Recipient of 14th District Political Scholarship
* GHK Leadership Program - outstanding academic achievements and leadership awards
* Outstanding Volunteer of the Year 2010, Springfield Community Center

Generic Resume

Robin Robine

213 Willow Street Anytown, Anystate 80111
Robin.Robine@gmail.com Cell phone: 999-999-9999 www.RobinRobine.net

EDUCATION
- University of Your State (UYS), Springfield
- Expected graduation December 2014
- Major: Business Administration Minor: Education
- Cumulative 3.2 GPA while working

HIGHLIGHTS OF QUALIFICATIONS
- Effective leader with ability to prioritize, delegate, and motivate
- Experienced in collaborating with others on group projects, as both leader and contributor
- Experienced Spanish translator, both oral and written
- Power user of MS Office Pro 2010 (Excel, Access, OneNote, Publisher, Visio)

RELEVANT COURSEWORK
- Macro and Micro Economics, Calculus, Statistics, Foundations of Education, Cognitive Psychology

RELEVANT EXPERIENCE
PROGRAM PLANNING & COORDINATING
- Collaborated with after-school teen program advisors and directors to establish and implement programs that were accepted by teen participants
- Development and delivery of four teen mentoring programs that became the model for three community centers
- Recruited and trained teens in peer mentoring techniques that resulted in 50% increase in retention and participation in the program
- Developed and delivered bilingual financial education program for non-English speakers, specifically addressing the concept and importance of saving and investing

NEEDS ASSESSMENT/ADVISING
- Administered and allocated funds for the teen counseling program, managing funds within budget
- Initiated investigation into the need for bullying prevention program and presented a report to school administrators
- Conducted bilingual survey, analyzed the results, and reported finding to program directors

EMPLOYMENT HISTORY
Aug. 2012 – Current Peer Advisor Student Service Program
Jun. 2012 – Oct. 2012 Security Monitor Summer Bridge
May 2011 – Jun. 2011 Civic Engagement Canvasser InnerCity Struggle
Mar. 2011 – Jun. 2011 Tutor/High School Counselor/Upward Bound

RELEVANT COMMUNITY AND VOLUNTEER EXPERIENCE
Jan. 2012 Philanthropy Chair, Pi Lambda Phi (Academic Fraternity)
Sept. 2011 Service Director, Springfield Community Center
Sept. 2011 Outreach Committee Member, Springfield Community Center
Jan. 2012 Extern at Children's Aid Society, Mytown, NX
Sept. 2011 Bilingual Tutor, XYZ Hall on campus
Sept. 2011 – May 2013 Co-President, Tingle Hall on campus

AWARDS and HONORS
- Recipient of full scholarship, ABC Scholarship Fund
- Recipient of 14th District Political Scholarship
- GHK Leadership Program - outstanding academic achievements and leadership awards
- Outstanding Volunteer of the Year 2010, Springfield Community Center

Notes

CHAPTER 6

Acing the Interview

STEP 1
PHONE
INTERVIEW

STEP 2
IN-PERSON
INTERVIEW

During the job interview, you will need all your "E³" skills. You will be meeting new people (by phone and in person), speaking about your qualifications and enthusiasm for the position, and demonstrating your entrepreneurial abilities by asking questions and showing that you are an "out of the box" thinker. Due to your great preparation, your actions and presence, you will show that you're engaging and can handle yourself well in a stressful interview situation.

You'll know you are successful when ... you are contacted by the employer and offered the job!

There are two types of interviews: telephone and in-person.

Both types of interview require preparation.

The first interview is generally by phone. It is used to narrow the field by asking some key questions. The phone interviewer is also trying to get a sense of who you are. If you make the cut, there will be at least one face-to-face interview.

I.   The phone interview

A phone interview can come any time after you click "Send." The recruiter or hiring manager may email you to set up a time to talk, or the recruiter may call, so it's best to be prepared. If you have the opportunity to schedule the call, choose a time when you will be in a quiet place and can give the call your full attention. Try to use a land line phone so you have good reception.

Prepare

- If you know the name of the organization, continue your research through the web and by asking people anything they know about the organization.

- Make notes about points you want to expand on. There may be an opportunity to address some of the soft skills that were part of the job posting.

- Review the **Interviewer Questions** at the end of this chapter. Practice answering them so you come across as knowledgeable, confident, articulate, and engaging.

- Have the job posting and your application (cover letter and resume) in front of you so you can refer to them.

- Interviewers will judge you based on the questions you ask them.

  ▲ **Don't** ask questions that could have been answered with a bit of web research.

  ▲ **Don't** ask about salary and benefits. This is not the appropriate time.

During the call

- If the call occurs without the benefit of scheduling, ask the interviewer for a few seconds to "shut the door" or "find a quiet place to talk." In those few seconds, try to put whatever was in your mind aside so you can fully concentrate.

- Stand up and smile during the call. The voice that comes through the phone will sound more engaging and enthusiastic.

- Ask for clarification when necessary, and think out your answers before responding. Avoid "ums" and "ers." If you need some time to think about an answer, say so – just don't do it too often or take too long. Remember to breathe when you're feeling nervous. It will help calm you.

- Express your interest in the position and your hope that you will have the opportunity to interview in person.

- Don't just answer a question with a one-word answer. Explain your answer but be very careful not to ramble on as some people tend to do when they get nervous. Keep your answers on topic and to the point. Be concise, informative and enthusiastic.

2. The face-to-face interview(s)

These can be either one on one, a panel interview or several different interviews back-to-back with multiple people.

It's also possible that an interview can take place over a meal. If this is the case, order something small and easy to eat. Never ask to take leftovers home.

Face-to-face interviews allow both sides to gain information and assess whether there is a good fit.

The interview process is where you start building the relationship and showcasing your value. Once you've built maximum value and received the job offer, you are in an excellent position to negotiate the best compensation package possible. (See Chapter 7.)

You will have your own criteria. While outwardly demonstrating that you are the best person for the job, inwardly you will be sizing up the people and environment to judge whether the workplace and the job are the right fit for you.

After the first interview, you may be called for at least one more interview.

Preparation

Whether the face-to-face interview is the first, second or third, preparation is similar.

- Make copies of your resume, transcript, references, and any forms you have been asked to complete to take along.

- Study your notes about the organization (see Chapter 5), and try to learn even more about it through research and networking. Explore the field in general so you can ask educated questions. Research competitors, stock values, source of funding (non-profits), geographic locations, and names of executives if available.

- Review the job posting and your resume and cover letter. Be ready to expand on the story of your connection to the organization's mission.

- Practice answering Interviewer Questions on page 141 with a friend, mentor or professional person.

- Prepare several true stories that expand on and validate the hard and soft skills you listed on your resume and cover letter.

- Prepare to ask appropriate questions. Here are some examples:

  - ▲ What is the biggest challenge facing your organization/industry/ field today?

  - ▲ What is the management style? How are decisions made?

  - ▲ What are some typical first-year assignments? What kind of training is given to new employees?

  - ▲ How is success measured in this position, division, organization?

  - ▲ How do you evaluate an employee's performance during the training period?

  - ▲ What quality do you look for in new hires? What skills are especially important in this position?

  - ▲ What are the challenges of this position?

  - ▲ Please describe typical first-year assignments.

  - ▲ Does your organization encourage further education?

  - ▲ Is there a career path for this position?

  - ▲ What are the next steps in the hiring process?

- As with the phone interview, DO NOT ask:

  - ▲ About information that you could easily find on the organization's website.

  - ▲ About salary and benefits until the position has been offered or this is brought up by the interviewer.

- Plan travel so you can arrive at least 15 minutes early. If possible, conduct a "dry run" so there are no surprises on the day of the interview.

- Make sure your clothes are appropriate and ready the night before (see Chapter 2).

- Get a good night's sleep.

Day of the interview

- Drink little or no coffee prior and during the interview. This makes some people talk too fast and it also causes dry mouth. Accept water if you're offered so you can also pause with a sip of water if you feel nervous.

- Use the same courtesy and enthusiasm with everyone you meet, beginning with the receptionist. At every step in the interview, you are being evaluated on your manners, personality and potential fit with the organization.

- Smile and make eye contact.

- Show your interest by sitting up straight and leaning slightly forward. Ask your prepared questions as they occur to you.

- Be prepared to be asked the same question by different people you meet. Be honest and consistent in your answers.

- Back up your answers with examples.

- Answer with the truth, but don't excessively embellish or feel the need to start at the very beginning. Keep your answers concise and to the point.

- If a question catches you off guard, acknowledge it as "a very good question," and ask for a moment to think about your response.

- If you are asked what salary you are expecting, it's always best to start off with a salary range based on your research, such as "my salary requirement is in the $40,000 – $50,000 range." If you don't have any idea of the expectations at your first discussion, you can also state that your salary requirements are flexible.

- Be aware of the energy you're picking up from the surroundings and the people you meet. Be thinking about whether this is an organization you want to join.

- Collect business cards from the people you meet so you know their names, positions and contact information, and you'll have the information to follow up.

- Very important: Express enthusiasm and interest in the job.

- Ask when you can expect to hear from the employer again.

- If an offer is made "on the spot," ask if you will get the offer in writing and take a day to consider it. (See Chapter 7 for steps in negotiation.)

Follow up

- Within 24 hours, write a short (no more than one-page) thank you letter or email to the decision maker. If you want the job, state your admiration for the organization and the people you met. State your interest in the position, and provide another piece of information about why you're the right person. Give specifics about how you can contribute.

- Also send an email to others you have met at the interview.

- If you think you don't want the job, send a thank you anyway, expressing your appreciation for the interviewer's time and consideration.

- If you do want the job but have not been contacted after five business days, call or email the employer. Think carefully about what you will say, but don't read it. Reiterate the main points in your note, and again express your interest. If you're transferred to voice mail, leave a message. Be sure to give your name and phone number clearly and slowly at the beginning of the message.

- If you make contact with the employer and he/she informs you that you are no longer being considered:

  ▲ Thank the employer for his/her time and consideration.

▲ Ask politely, "To help me in my future job search, would you please tell me what were the factors that led to your decision?" Then listen carefully. Thank the employer again for this important feedback.

▲ Depending on the reason why you were passed over, ask if there are any other openings that you might fill – or ask if they would consider you for other potential positions.

Example of interviewer questions with possible types of appropriate responses

Interviewer Question	Possible response
What are your greatest strengths?	As a recent graduate of Smith University, I have benefited from the latest thinking in the field of ..., I work very well in teams, both leading and contributing ... (give example).
What are your greatest weaknesses?	Choose one that is not of major consequence, and the steps you've taken to overcome it. For example: If you have a history of needing to sleep in, say something like: "Now that I'm out of school and no longer have to stay up late studying, I'm going to bed earlier, and I set my alarm and get up early so I can take a run. And I'm surprising myself because I'm really beginning to enjoy early mornings." Whatever you say should be true. Or "I used to leave deadlines to the last minute, but when I realized the consequences impacted others, I changed that and now I put everything in my calendar in advance and I feel good about not stressing myself and others.
Tell me about yourself.	Draw from your bio (See Chapter 5)
What salary are you seeking?	This is where preparation is vital. Some positions can be researched on a website such as www.salary.com. You can state your understanding that the salary range for this type of position generally is between $____ and $____. Don't start too low or ask for an amount that is unreasonably high for this type of position. You'll need to do your research and homework (see Chapter 7).

Chapter 6 Reminders

Section 1: The phone interviews

☐ Prepare by reviewing the job posting, your response, and practicing answers.

☐ Shut out other distractions.

☐ Smile and respond enthusiastically.

☐ Ask your prepared or other relevant questions that may come up for you.

☐ Ask about next steps and state your interest in the position – show enthusiasm!

Section 2: The face-to-face interviews

☐ Conduct further research on the organization and the field in general.

☐ Practice answering the interview questions.

☐ Make copies of your resume, references, transcripts to bring along if needed.

☐ Arrive early – well rested, well dressed, and fed.

☐ Answer every question truthfully and succinctly.

☐ Ask questions about the organization and the position.

☐ Pay attention to the environment and what you hear so you can decide if the job and organization appear to be a good fit for you.

☐ Ask about the next steps in the hiring process.

☐ Follow up with email, thank you notes, and phone calls as appropriate. Be persistent, but not a pest.

Example Interviewer Questions

The following are examples of common interview questions. Prepare by practicing with a friend, mentor or when possible, with a professional.

- Tell me about yourself.

- Walk me through your resume. Focus on relevant work or course experience to the position.

- How did you choose your university? your major?

- What is your favorite/least favorite class? Why?

- What is your approach to work?

- How will you handle the pressure of maintaining your academics and the responsibility of a job/internship at the same time?

- What are your strengths?

- What are your weaknesses?

- What do you know about this organization?

- Why do you think you would like this organization and this type of work?

- How do your work experiences relate to this position?

- What interests you most about this position?

- What are the 2 or 3 things you are looking for in a job. Why are they important to you?

- In your opinion, what are the personal characteristics necessary for success in this field?

- Where would you like to be in your career five years from now?

- What is your ideal organization to work for?

- Why should we hire you? What skills and abilities do you bring to this position?

- What did you like least about your last job?

- When have you been most satisfied in your work?

- What can you do for us that other candidates can't?

- Where would you like to be in 5 years? (Your answer is important. You don't want to say at another organization, or in graduate school.)

- What were the responsibilities of your last position? Why did you leave?

- Why did you leave your last job?

- What do you know about this industry?

- Are you willing to relocate?

- What was the last project you headed up, and what was its outcome?

- Give me an example of a time you exceeded expectations/did more than what was required?

- Can you describe a time when your work was criticized? How did you handle the criticism?

- Tell me about a time you didn't meet a project deadline. What happened/what was the outcome? What, if anything, would you have done differently?

- Describe the most complex project you've ever led or worked on.

- Give me examples of how you managed a team through a difficult time.

- Have you ever been on a team or project where people were not pulling their own weight? How did you handle it?

- Tell me about a time when you had to give someone difficult feedback. How did you handle it?

- When in the past have you received direction from multiple supervisors. How did you feel about it, and how did you handle it?

- What is your greatest failure, and what did you learn from it? (Focus more on the learning with this answer.)

- Give an example of when you were totally committed to a task.

- Think about your favorite work experience – a time or event that gave you great personal satisfaction. Describe it, and tell why it was important.

- Think about an actual intense or pressure-packed situation. Can you tell me about it and describe your role and how you handled it, and what was accomplished?

- How do you inspire/motivate people? Give me an example of who you helped/how you helped.

- What types of problems do you like to solve?

- Define leadership, and tell me about a time when you have been successful as a leader.

- Describe a situation in which there was a conflict between a task or assignment you had to complete and a personal situation that required your time. What did you do?

- Describe the best manager you've ever had. Why was this person the best?

- What irritates you about other people, and how do you deal with it?

- If I were your supervisor and asked you to do something that you disagreed with, what would you do?

- What was the most difficult period in your life, and how did you deal with it? (Keep this short.)

- What is a common misperception people have about you?

- Give me an example of a time you did something wrong. How did you handle it?

- What irritates you about other people, and how do you deal with it?

- Tell me about a time where you had to deal with conflict on the job.

- If you were at a business lunch and you ordered a rare steak and they brought it to you well done, what would you do?

- If you found out your company was doing something against the law, like fraud, what would you do?

- Tell me about a difficult decision you made where you stood by your ethics, even though others did not agree with you.

- What assignment was too difficult for you, and how did you resolve the issue?

- What's the most difficult decision you've made in the last two years, and how did you come to that decision?

- Describe how you would handle a situation if you were required to finish multiple tasks by the end of the day, and there was no conceivable way that you could finish them.

- How would you go about establishing your credibility quickly with the team?

- How long will it take for you to make a significant contribution?

- What do you see yourself doing within the first 30 days of this job?

- If selected for this position, can you describe your strategy for the first 90 days?

- What are you looking for in terms of career advancement?

- How do you want to improve yourself in the next year?

- What kind of goals would you have in mind if you got this job?

- If I were to ask your last supervisor to provide information about your performance, what would he/she answer?

- What salary are you seeking?

- What's your salary history?

- How would you describe your work style?

- What would be your ideal working situation?

- What do you look for in terms of a work culture?

- Give examples of ideas you've had or implemented.

- What techniques and tools do you use to keep yourself organized?

- If you had to choose one, would you consider yourself a big-picture person or a detail-oriented person?

- Tell me about your proudest achievement.

- Who was your favorite manager and why?

- What do you think of your previous boss?

- Was there a person in your career who really made a difference?

- What kind of personality do you work best with and why?

- What are you most proud of?

- What do you like to do?

- What are your lifelong dreams?

- What is your personal mission statement?

- What are three positive things your last boss would say about you?

- What negative thing would your last boss say about you?

- What three character traits would your friends use to describe you?

- What are three positive character traits you don't have?

- If you were interviewing someone for this position, what traits would you look for?

- List five words that describe your character.

- What is your greatest fear?

- What is your biggest regret and why?

- What's the most important thing you learned in school?

- What will you miss about your present/last job?

- What is your greatest achievement outside of work?

- What are the qualities of a good leader? A bad leader?

- Do you think a leader should be feared or liked?

- How do you feel about taking no for an answer?

- Tell me the difference between good and exceptional.

- Do you drive or take public transportation?

- There's no right or wrong answer, but if you could be anywhere in the world right now, where would you be?

- What's the last book you read?

- What magazines do you like?

- What's the best movic you've seen in the last year?

- What would you do if you won the lottery?

- Who are your heroes?

- What do you like to do for fun?

- What do you do in your spare time?

- What is your favorite memory from childhood?

- Do you have any questions for me?

CHAPTER 7
Negotiating the Job Agreement

The final step in the hiring process is the negotiation of your employment. If this is your first professional job, your temptation may be to sign immediately. It's often worth it to take some time to consider and potentially ask for a change to the terms.

You'll know you're successful in negotiating the contract when ... the agreement or contract is signed by both parties, there is a win-win, and your new employer appreciates the entrepreneurial and engaging attributes you have demonstrated throughout the process.

The meaning of "negotiate"

In terms of the job offer, negotiation is a collaborative process in which the two parties arrive at a mutually agreeable contract that benefits both. It should be the first of many business-focused conversations between you and your employer in which both parties are invested in the welfare of the other. What often gets in the way of rewarding win-win conversations is the fear of rejection or potential conflict. Even in a tough job market, when the employer wants you, there is usually something you can negotiate.

Negotiating is a learned skill that needs to be developed. This chapter covers:

- The dynamics behind the employment contract conversation

- How to make terms win-win

- How to seal the deal

About

85%

of hiring managers don't make their best offer first.

I. The dynamics behind the employment contract conversation

If you are new to offers of employment – here are some things you need to know:

- You have some leverage.

- You are receiving the offer because you have been considered to be the best candidate for the job. This gives you room for negotiation. Most employers invest a lot of time and energy finding the right candidate. They understand that they must offer competitive salaries and benefits and are unlikely to rescind the offer when their #1 choice makes a good faith attempt to negotiate the terms of employment.

- You don't have to agree and sign immediately.

- Most employers expect you to request time to consider the offer. It's reasonable to ask for up to a week to make your decision. Be sure to express your enthusiasm about being offered the position and working for the organization or company.

- The days following a job offer are important to you. Once the offer is in your hands (or on your computer) use your time to think and do research.

- Employers typically make beginning offers at the lower end of the salary range.

Surveys show that about 85% of hiring managers don't make their best offer first. The employer typically makes an offer based on the range in their budget. Employers know that candidates may choose to negotiate, so they start on the low end. You have an advantage because the employer wants you – and respects people with an understanding of their value in terms of the market rate of compensation. You can increase your perceived value by being entrepreneurial in your negotiations – as long as you do it in a very professional way.

2. How to make terms win-win

Salary, benefits, work hours and responsibilities can be negotiable.

Negotiate salary

Even before you receive the offer, it's wise to research pay ranges by position and industry. This is where the work you performed on salaries "pays off." Look online for surveys to determine average salary. Study similar job descriptions both within and outside of the industry and organization. If the position is in a different geographic area, do your research and use salary calculators to factor in cost-of-living expenses to estimate a reasonable salary in your location. You also need to be considering your salary requirements. How much money do you need to manage financial obligations and live comfortably?

Once you have the offer, you are in a position to negotiate. It is always important to be patient. Counteroffers are typically about 10 – 15% of the original offer. Come up with three figures: (a) a minimum number that you can accept based on what you need and want, (b) a realistic midpoint number, and (c) a dream salary figure that is also within the range of reality. It's always easier to negotiate down.

Your negotiation range should come from your midpoint to your dream salary. When you have your salary range, you can adjust your requirements appropriately. If the employer provides you with a range of $45k – $55k a year, for example, you can come back with: "I was thinking about $55k - $57k, which means we are in a similar range and my ideal salary is $57k. Is there flexibility at the top of your range?"

This is the appropriate time to gain the information needed. If you are lucky enough to have multiple offers or other interviews scheduled, definitely let the employer know this as well.

If the offer is a specific dollar amount, mention your midpoint to maximum range. This enables you to negotiate down. You also should demonstrate your worth by saying something like, "Having compared my background with industry standards and knowing my work ethic, I feel my worth is in the range of $X to $Y. Don't you agree?" If they agree but cannot pay within that range, ask what they have in mind with respect to responsibilities, or ask "Is that the best you can do?" Some supervisors and employers are limited by budget constraints. There may not have enough money in the budget to meet your salary expectations. If this is so, ask yourself two questions:

- "Are the company culture, benefits, and co-workers worth more to me than my ideal salary?"

- "If I accept this lower salary, will I be able to pay my bills?" Be sure to consider your commute time and expenses, as well as clothes or equipment, and any expected work-related travel.

Even if the offer isn't what you expected, you still have options. You can ask about a 60-, 90-, or 120-day performance review tying it to an increase in salary. If you don't ask, the employer probably won't offer.

Negotiate benefits

Sometimes the benefits can be as important to you as the salary. A complete understanding of the facts is critical to your successful final negotiation. Be sure you understand all the benefits within the compensation package such as health, dental, vision, disability, life insurance, paid vacation and sick leave, retirement plans, profit-sharing and/or bonuses. Find out details about vacation, sick time and any other benefit programs such as a continuing education allowance, commute credit allowance, sabbaticals, or a travel program. Depending on your lifestyle or domestic commitments, work hour flexibility may be important to you. And there are other benefits besides salary – such as travel reimbursements or moving expenses.

Negotiate responsibilities

If you will be taking on more responsibility from a previous job or more responsibility than was originally discussed, or if you will be working full time rather than part time, the salary should generally be increased for that.

Know your own bottom line – other things to consider

Everyone's personal circumstances are different. Take time to review the pros and cons. Making a list is always helpful. Take the time to thoroughly evaluate the offer. During the time you have asked to consider the offer, do the following:

- Talk to mentors you know who can be objective and knowledgeable.

- Consider all aspects of the job and whether you think you can work effectively with your future supervisor. Take time to reflect on your "gut feeling" based on what you know about the company and your interactions with the supervisor during the interview. Is the supervisor confrontational? Hands-off or hands-on, and which typically works best for you? How do you expect different viewpoints will be handled?

- When you have questions, make a list and ask to speak with the employer again – being careful to limit the number of contacts to no more than two times.

- Consider other job offers you have received or might be receiving. If there is another employer of interest from whom an offer is pending, contact that employer and let him/her know that you have received another offer and when you must make a decision. Having two offers at the same time can greatly increase your negotiating power.

3. How to seal the deal

When you're at peace with the final offer, contact the employer. Verbally state the agreed salary and benefits and provide the date when you can begin working.

Get it in writing

It is customary to receive an employment contract or letter of hire, which outlines all of the details of your salary, benefits and work hours. Do not begin work without written confirmation of all the details to which you both have agreed. Verbal offers sometimes can be withdrawn, and terms of employment, salary, and benefits can change. If the employer does not provide a contract in writing, create a confirmation letter or email of your own, outlining all of the terms that were mutually agreed on.

By being prepared and gaining experience with negotiating, you'll build your confidence and demonstrate great communication and relationship building.

Chapter 7 Reminders

Section 1: The dynamics behind the employment contract conversation

- ❐ You have some leverage.
- ❐ You don't have to agree and sign immediately.
- ❐ Employers typically begin offers at the lower end of the salary range.

Section 2: How to make terms win-win

- ❐ Negotiate salary.
- ❐ Negotiate benefits and other perks.
- ❐ Know your own bottom line.

Section 3: How to seal the deal

- ❐ Get it in writing.

You've taken the steps to **Get The Job You Love!** When you continue to show up prepared, confident and enthusiastic you'll be a great candidate and a fantastic employee. Hopefully you too will help others along the way.

Go get 'em!!!

Go to **www.thejobyoulove.com** for more tips and information. We'd like to have your questions and comments.

Made in the USA
Lexington, KY
25 September 2012